DANCE
The Higher Call

**God's Glorious Mandate for
Transforming Your Life,
Reflecting His Son,
and Revealing His Glory**

DANCE
The Higher Call

**God's Glorious Mandate for
Transforming Your Life,
Reflecting His Son,
and Revealing His Glory**

DR. PAMELA HARDY

BASAR PUBLISHING

DANCE: THE HIGHER CALL
GOD'S GLORIOUS MANDATE FOR TRANSFORMING YOUR LIFE, REFLECTING HIS SON, AND REVEALING HIS GLORY

© 2015 by Dr. Pamela Hardy

Scripture quotations, unless noted otherwise, are taken from the King James Bible Version.

ISBN 978-1-942013-83-9

Printed in the United States of America.

Cover Design: Eric Culberson

Editors: Rekesha Pittman, ShaVonne Thomas

Interior Formatting: Rekesha Pittman

PRAISE FOR
"DANCE: The Higher Call"

I don't know anyone who is more qualified to extend this "Higher Call" to dancers and ministers of worship than Dr. Pamela Hardy. I have traveled with Pamela to worship conferences throughout the USA and overseas, and have seen her excellence in character, teaching anointing and revelation. Pamela has been one of the "Mothers" and innovators of dance ministry for over 25 years, and she has led the way in the prophetic dance movement throughout that time.

It takes a visionary with a true worshiper's heart to maintain such excellence for this length of time. This book reflects the wisdom, revelation and creativity that Pamela has walked/danced in throughout her ministry.

I am honored to recommend "Dance: The Higher Call" to dancers, worship ministers, pastors and worshipers of all denominations and generations. It is one of those "must read" titles that will prove to be an invaluable resource for your worship personnel–time and time again.

Vivien Hibbert

Author of "Prophetic Worship" and "Praise Him"

Founder of the Worship Arts Conservatory
www.vivienhibbert.com

www.theheartoftheworshiper.blogspot.com

Dr. Pamela Hardy has blended scripture with experience in a prolific manner. Her love and comprehension of the Word as well as application is to be commended. She challenges dance artists to move forward not only in skill but in righteousness so that the purity of the ministry will shine forth and glorify God.

Elizabeth Hairston-Mc Burrows, Ph.D.

Founder - Rose of Sharon School of Dance
Founder - Women With A Call International
Founder - The Apostolic-Prophetic Connection

www.drelizabethhairston.com

In her book, "Dance: The Higher Call," Dr. Pamela Hardy speaks articulately to the one who has "ears to hear and eyes to see." This is a book replete with solid biblical teaching and more importantly, practical application.

Dr. Pamela is an activator! When studied and applied, this book will change your life!

Yvonne Diez Peters

Without End Ministries
Tampa, Florida

Dr. Pamela Hardy's impact in the dance community is a global phenomenon. Her passion for authentic, powerful movement extends far beyond the dance floor. Investing in the training, equipping and empowerment of worship artists across the world has become a signature of Dr. Pamela's life and legacy.

"Dance: The Higher Call" will compel the reader to make the necessary adjustments required to soar beyond the ordinary. If you realize that there is a higher call... If you are willing to accept a greater mandate... If you are yearning to move in a way that changes lives forever, this book is the answer. Accept the call!

Rekesha Pittman

Publishing Coach - Eagles International Authors Institute

Author of several books, including:
"Company Keepers: Dance Ministry Daily "
"Dance Leaders Advance"
"7 Steps to a Divine Dance Company" and
"Of Them That Danced: Moving Through The Scriptures"

www.rekeshapittman.com

TABLE OF CONTENTS

The High Calling of God

Introduction

Section 1

Section 2

THE HIGH CALLING OF GOD

1. If God has called you to be really like Jesus in all your spirit, He will draw you into a life of crucifixion and humility. He will put on you such demands of obedience that He will not allow you to follow other Christians, and in many ways He will seem to let other good people do things which He will not let you do.

2. Other Christians and ministers who seem very religious and useful may push themselves, pull wires and work schemes to carry out their plans, but you cannot do it. If you attempt it, you will meet with such failure and rebuke from the Lord as to make you sorely penitent.

3. Others can brag about themselves, their work, their success, or their writings, but the Holy Spirit will not allow you to do any such thing. If you begin it, He will lead you into such deep mortification that will make you despise yourself and all your good works.

4. Others will be allowed to succeed in making great sums of money or having a legacy left to them or in having luxuries. But God may supply you daily because He wants you to have something far better than gold, and that is a helpless dependence on Him, that He may have the privilege of providing your needs day by day out of the unseen treasury.

5. The Lord may let others be honored and put forward but keep you hidden away in obscurity because He wants to produce some choice, fragrant fruit for His coming glory, which can only be produced in the shade.

6. God will let others be great, but keep you small. He will let others do a work for Him and get the credit for it, but He will make you work and toil on without knowing how much you are doing. Then to make your work still more precious, He will let others get the credit for the work which you have done, and this will make your reward ten times greater when Jesus comes.

7. The Holy Spirit will put a strict watch on you, with a jealous love, and will rebuke you for little words and feelings or for wasting your time, which other Christians never seem distressed over.

8. So make up your mind that God is an infinite Sovereign, and has a right to do as He pleases with His own. He will not explain to you a thousand things which may puzzle your reason in His dealings with you. God will take you at your word; and if you absolutely will yourself to be His slave, He will wrap you up in a jealous love and let other people say and do many things that you cannot do or say. Settle it forever, that you are to deal directly with the Holy Spirit. Also that He is to have the privilege of tying your tongue or chaining your hand or closing your eyes, in ways that others are not dealt with.

9. Now when you are so possessed with the loving God that you are, in your secret heart, pleased and delighted over this peculiar personal, private, jealous guardianship and management of the Holy Spirit over your life, you will have found the vestibule of heaven.

(Source Unknown)

INTRODUCTION

"But what things were gain to me, those I counted loss for Christ. Yea doubtless, and I count all things but loss for the excellency of the knowledge of Christ Jesus my Lord: for whom I have suffered the loss of all things, and do count them but dung, that I may win Christ, And be found in him, not having mine own righteousness, which is of the law, but that which is through the faith of Christ, the righteousness which is of God by faith: That I may know him, and the power of his resurrection, and the fellowship of his sufferings, being made conformable unto his death; If by any means I might attain unto the resurrection of the dead. Not as though I had already attained, either were already perfect: but I follow after, if that I may apprehend that for which also I am apprehended of Christ Jesus. Brethren, I count not myself to have apprehended: but this one thing I do, forgetting those things which are behind, and reaching forth unto those things which are before, I press toward the mark for the prize of the high calling of God in Christ Jesus. Let us therefore, as many as be perfect, be thus minded..."

— Philippians 3:7-15 (KJV)

If anyone could think he had arrived, it would have been the Apostle Paul. But he always kept in mind that he had not arrived yet. He didn't want to rest on what he had already achieved. Paul was a man who received numerous visions of the Lord. He had been caught up into heaven and had seen things that no other living person had seen.

Yet, Paul rejected all confidence in the flesh and those things that were gain to him, he counted loss for Christ. Paul knew that we could not please God in the energies of the flesh. He counted all things as loss in view of the excellence of the knowledge of Christ Jesus. It wasn't so much that those things were worthless in themselves, but compared to the greatness of the excellence of the knowledge of Christ Jesus, they meant nothing.

Paul wrote this letter from a Roman prison. He could truly say that he had suffered the loss of all things. He counted them as rubbish. Paul used strong language. Literally, Paul considered them as excrement—as dung; not only as worthless, but as offensive.

The ancient Greek word for rubbish had one of two uses. It could describe excrement from the body or table scraps that were fit only to be thrown to the dogs. The word rubbish means the vilest dross or the worst excrement. The word shows how utterly insignificant all things are as compared to winning (gaining) Christ.

This is the requirement for being found in Him, having only the righteousness of God that comes through faith in Christ. Let the cry of our heart be to know Him, the power of His resurrection, and the fellowship of His sufferings. Let us embrace the process of being conformed to His death, that we may attain to the resurrection. This was the cry of Paul's heart. Paul wanted Jesus, not self.

"To know Jesus is not the same as knowing His historical life; it is not the same as knowing correct doctrines regarding Jesus; it is not the same as knowing His moral example, and it is not the same as knowing His great work on our behalf.

We can say that we know someone because we recognize him: because we can distinguish what is different about him compared to other people.

We can say that we know someone because we are acquainted with what he does; we know the baker because we get our bread from him.

We can say that we know someone because we actually converse with him; we are on speaking terms with that person.

We can say that we know someone because we spend time in his house and with his family.

We can say that we know someone because we have committed our life to him and live with him every day, sharing every circumstance as in a marriage."

-Author Unknown

But do we really know Him?

> "They tell me he is a refiner, that he cleanses from spots; he has washed me in his precious blood, and to that extent I know him. They tell me that he clothes the naked; he hath covered me with a garment of righteousness, and to that extent I know him. They tell me that he is a breaker, and that he breaks fetters, he has set my soul at liberty, and therefore I know him. They tell me that he is a king and that he reigns over sin; he hath subdued my enemies beneath his feet, and I know him in that character. They tell me he is a shepherd: I know him for I am his sheep. They say he is a door: I have entered in through him, and I know him as a door. They say he is food: my spirit feeds on him as on the bread of heaven, and, therefore, I know him as such." (Spurgeon)

Knowing Jesus means knowing this power, the new life that is imparted to us now, not when we die. He wants us to know the power of Christ's resurrection in an experiential way. The same power that raised Christ from the dead dwells in us (Romans 8:11).

The revelations Paul received allowed him to write some of the most life-changing words ever written. He said he still had much to attain to in order to eagerly take, seize, possess and overtake that which he was also eagerly taken, seized, possessed and overtaken of

Christ. Yet he did not consider himself to have already apprehended. Beloved, have you been taken, seized, possessed and overtaken by Christ?

Paul realized that he had not arrived. There was only one option for him. He had to press on. There was no turning back. His attitude was, "I need to keep stretching for that which is ahead and pressing toward the mark for the prize of the high calling."

Paul said there was "one thing" that he needed to do, but that "one thing" required a 3-step process:

1. Forget those things that are behind.
2. Reach forth to the things that are before.
3. Press toward the mark for the prize of the high calling of God in Christ Jesus.

(1) Concerning your past—leave it there! It is your past, not your present. Yesterday is gone. Since God does not bring up our past, why do we? He tells us that once we confess our sins, He is faithful and just to forgive us and cleanse us from all unrighteousness (1 John1:9). He throws our sin "into the depths of the sea" (Micah 7:19)! Leave your past in the past and keep moving forward. Forget the things that are behind.

(2) Reach forward to what lies ahead. Move forward toward the future. No matter what, don't stop.

(3) The upward call of God has to do with every part of our lives and everything we do—how we conduct ourselves in private and in public; how we spend our time and money; how we serve the Lord—should all be done with an awareness of the presence of God. We need to adopt a holy dissatisfaction with anything that is not pleasing to the Lord.

Answer the invitation. Let Jesus overtake you to make you holy and perfect before Him. Let Jesus overtake you to conform you into His image. Don't allow distractions. Focus on the prize.

The prize is the call itself. The prize is the upward call of God. It came from the heart of God. It's far above our own thoughts. He is the prize.

> *"The eyes of your understanding being enlightened; that ye may know what is the hope of his calling, and what the riches of the glory of his inheritance in the saints."* - Ephesians 1:18

You have been invited. What will your answer be?

SECTION

1

Chapter 1
Called to Show Forth His Praise

If you like being a "normal" Christian, this message is not for you. If you are satisfied with where you are, this message is not for you. If you are afraid to rock the boat, this message is not for you. If you want to keep in step with this world, this message is not for you.

If you will take the words of this book and apply them daily with an earnest heart and full surrender, it will require you to change. You have been chosen by a Holy, righteous God who has called you out of darkness to reflect the beauty of His holiness.

> *"But ye are a chosen generation, a royal priesthood, an holy nation, a peculiar people; that ye should shew forth the praises of him who hath called you out of darkness into his marvellous light."* - 1 Peter 2

Question: What's the purpose of dance ministry?

Answer: To show forth the praises of the One who has called you out of darkness into His marvelous light.

Showing forth His praises has to do with the point of origin of movement. He is the source of all life. The only things that don't move are dead things. Everything

God created has life and life manifests through movement.

He has called you out of darkness, out of obscurity, into His marvelous light so you can bring light to darkness and reflect His image. You must abide in Him and stay hidden in Him because it's by His light that others can see. So you are a light reflector.

In essence, you are called out of darkness to show forth the glory, beauty and majesty of God so others can see who He is. Therefore, you must be the sights of God for others to see. To see means to behold. When people see you, they should see Jesus.

Pure dances of light are for the mature, for those who can express who God is in them and what God has done in them. Only free people can free people. The days of dancing without being free must end now. Those days are over. Through you, God wants to express His majesty and His glory. You must be the sights of God for all to see.

In order for us be a visual demonstration, we must let Him purify us. We cannot take dances from the world and call them holy. They will not produce the sights of God. They will not produce the life of God. They are counterfeit and often deceiving because they might look like the real thing but we must discern the pure from the impure. We can redeem them, but we must not copy them.

Have we really begun to dance? Can we express in the natural, what God is saying and doing in the Spirit?

Can we release pure dances that liberate the spirit and set the captives free? Do we have the anointing that will break oppression, deliver people from fear and guilt and bring people out of their captivity? When you minister in dance, will we still see Him?

In the book of John, Jesus told His disciples that to see Him meant to see the Father.

> "Thomas saith unto him, Lord, we know not whither thou goest; and how can we know the way? Jesus saith unto him, I am the way, the truth, and the life: no man cometh unto the Father, but by me. If ye had known me, ye should have known my Father also: and from henceforth ye know him, and have seen him. Philip saith unto him, Lord, shew us the Father, and it sufficeth us. Jesus saith unto him, Have I been so long time with you, and yet hast thou not known me, Philip? he that hath seen me hath seen the Father; and how sayest thou then, Shew us the Father?" - John 14:5-9

We should be able to say the same thing. Our lives should display God. When people see us, they should see our God.

> "Then answered Jesus and said unto them, Verily, verily, I say unto you, The Son can do nothing of himself, but what he seeth the

Father do: for what things soever he doeth, these also doeth the Son likewise." - John 5:19

Jesus always displayed the sights of God because His eyes were always on God. His focus was always on doing the will of the Father so others could see the Father. If Jesus did not see it from the Father, He did not display it in the earth.

What are you doing when no one is watching? Are you still revealing Christ? Can God be seen through your actions?

Every part of our lives should reveal Christ and show forth the sights of God. God makes the minister and the ministry one. Revealing Christ is not limited to when we minister in dance. We must reveal Christ in the mall, in our home and on our job. We must show forth His praises so others can see Him!

Let's be responsible stewards of the gifts God has given us. Overall, as we observe the ministry of dance, we have been blessed but we have not even yet begun to really dance. Why do I say that? Because God is more concerned about who you are becoming than what you are doing.

He did not bring you into the Kingdom to become a famous dancer. He brought you into the Kingdom to be conformed to the image of His Son. That's how we become the sights of God. We often try to do what we have not yet become. God wants dances that minister spirit to spirit, not flesh to flesh. We should be clothed

4

with Christ so people see only that which comes from His Spirit.

God has a high call on those who dance His dances. Everything belongs to God, therefore, the dance is His. Every movement is His. Every step is His. Every wave of the arm or turning of the body... it all belongs to Him. He has a higher purpose than we have seen.

He has allowed us to dance, but it's a new season. You can no longer allow time for people, places and things that take you away from purity. Playtime is over. People are living in iniquity in the church, dancing in their iniquity, dancing in their sin, filled with pride, centered on self. There is too much of the world in the church, too much of the world in the dance ministry.

It's time to get serious. It's time for the true ministers of dance to arise—those who are not afraid to go through the refiner's fire to a place of purity for the purpose of being the sights of God to show forth His praise.

Commit to follow after that which is pure. Attach yourself only to those who are pure. God's people are not recognized by social acceptability or self-advertised success. God's people are not recognized by their outward appearance or by beautiful dances. God's people are known by their purity, their humility, and by His grace working in their hearts.

This is the higher call.

Chapter 2

Called to the Refiner's Fire

God is doing a new thing in the hearts of His people. Many have forgotten the true purpose of what God has called them to do. The cares of this world have distracted His servants and turned people away from the heart of God. But the remnant continues to stand, confess, pray and believe that God's promises shall come to pass.

God is gathering a people who will allow Him to re-awaken and rekindle the burning embers within their hearts. He's has called us to be refreshed and refined by His Fire.

> *"Behold, I will send my messenger, and he shall prepare the way before me: and the Lord, whom ye seek, shall suddenly come to his temple, even the messenger of the covenant, whom ye delight in: behold, he shall come, saith the LORD of hosts. But who may abide the day of his coming? and who shall stand when he appeareth? for he is like a refiner's fire, and like fullers' soap: And he shall sit as a refiner and purifier of silver: and he shall purify the sons of Levi, and purge them as gold and silver, that they may offer unto the LORD an offering in righteousness. Then shall the offering of Judah and Jerusalem be pleasant*

unto the LORD, as in the days of old, and as in former years." - Malachi 3:1-4

Our first call is to love and worship a God who is holy. The ministry of dance is a manifestation in response to that call.

One who ministers in dance must go through the fire of the refiner. The minister must be purified. Once the MINISTER surrenders to the refining process, the MINISTRY of dance accomplishes its true purpose in the earth.

What does it mean to be refined? Refining is the process of reducing the impurities in a substance. Faith is the substance. The opposite of faith is fear. Perfect love casts out all fear. God IS Love. Since He is Love, it only makes sense that the One who loves you is the One who also refines you so that you can become the same faith substance of His Son.

The fire belongs to the refiner. It is He who determines the type of fire that is needed and the length of time that the vessel needs to remain in the fire to be conformed to the image that the refiner desires. Let's look a little closer at the word "refined."

Refined means:
1. To bring to a pure state; free from impurities.
2. To purify from what is coarse, vulgar, or debasing; to make elegant or cultured.
3. To bring to a finer state or form by purifying.

4. To make more precise
5. To make fine distinctions in thought or language.

Without this refining, we will not be able to offer to the Lord an offering in righteousness that will be pleasing to Him. Pleasant offerings are those that are agreeable with His nature and character... Offerings that are void of self... Offerings that are sweet offerings... Those are the offerings that He takes pleasure in.

Allow Holy Spirit to show you what impurities are in you that need to be brought to the top and removed so that His righteousness can shine through and His glory can be revealed.

The messenger of the covenant is coming. Make no mistake. He is coming and coming to His temple suddenly!

John Piper writes: The Bible says that God is like a refiner's fire. It "does not say that He is like a forest fire, or like an incinerator's fire. It says that He is like a refiner's fire. A forest fire destroys indiscriminately. An incinerator consumes completely."

> "I the LORD do not change; therefore you, O sons of Jacob, are not consumed—you are not destroyed." - Malachi 3:6

Piper continues, "He is a refiner's fire, and that makes all the difference. A refiner's fire does not destroy everything like a forest fire. A refiner's fire does not consume completely like the fire of an incinerator. A refiner's fire refines. It purifies. It melts down the bar of silver or gold, separates out the impurities that ruin its value, burns them up, and leaves the silver and gold intact. He is like a refiner's fire.

It does say FIRE. And therefore purity and holiness will always be a dreadful thing. There will always be a proper "fear and trembling" in the process of becoming pure.

Serving God should never be taken lightly. It is not a plaything. God makes the ministry and the minister one. You cannot separate them. You are not anointed when you are serving as a minister of dance and then suddenly not anointed throughout the course of your daily life. The ministry of dance is not meant to be for entertainment. It's not meant to be a social club. It is meant to have the power to change hearts, lives and atmospheres. That's why our passion for purity must remain constant. It should never be put on the back burner. Ministry of dance is important and it should never be treated flippantly.

He is like fire and fire is serious. You don't play around with it. The furnace of affliction in the life of God's child is always for refinement, never for destruction. We are impure by nature. God will have no impurities in the Kingdom. Therefore, He must be a refiner's fire.

The words refine, purify and purge all express the same concept of cleansing and removing imperfections by a process—a process that each dance minister must undergo if we are to bring offerings of righteousness.

Until 500 BC, silver was considered to be the most valuable metal on earth. During Solomon's reign, gold replaced silver as the most precious metal. Gold and silver share some important properties that explain why they are viewed so highly, not only in the past, but also today. You will see some obvious spiritual parallels.

Principle A: Silver is the second most malleable metal next to gold. This makes them both very easy to fashion and mold.

Spiritual Parallel: Is your heart pliable in the Master's hand or do you have a hard heart and resist His instructions?

Principle B: Both have a brilliant metallic lustre or shine that does not tarnish or corrode.

Spiritual Parallel: Are you staying in His presence so that you can continue to shine for Him or do you continue to bring forth that which is old and stale? Do you allow the cares of this world to tarnish who you are?

Principle C: The reason gold and silver do not tarnish or corrode is because they do not react with the atmosphere. Even at high temperatures, gold and silver still remain inert.

Spiritual Parallel: Do you react to the atmosphere around you or are you an atmosphere-changer because you have allow the Holy Spirit to consume who you are so He can shine through?

The refining of gold and silver follow the same process. The impure gold or silver is placed along with pieces of lead, into a crucible-type vessel. It is then placed into a furnace where the metal melts and mixes with the lead, forming a molten liquid mass of metal.

Air, under force, is then blown onto the surface of the molten metal while still in the furnace. The lead, once it comes in contact with the blowing air, reacts, then circulates throughout the molten metal. This circulating, reacted lead then absorbs all the other metal impurities to form a mixture called dross, which vaporizes or floats to the surface. The floating dross is then subsequently blown over the edge of the crucible by the blasting air and is consumed by the furnace. The gold or silver is then left behind in the crucible—free of all impurities.

Why is this important for us? Because the ministry of dance must come forth from a pure vessel, free from impurities. We must cry out for that which is pure, that which is real and authentic, that which comes from heaven. Only that which is real will change our hearts and effect the earth realm.

So then it remains for us to be like pure silver or gold and not like the dross. If we are to be pure, then we must put away sin and live a life defined by the purity of God's Word.

To be pure, we must repent. We cannot continually lean to our own understanding, live as we please, and think we will be pleasing to God. We must give up every right we think we have to ourselves.

> "Flee also youthful lusts; but pursue right-eousness, faith, love, peace with those who call on the Lord out of a pure heart."
>
> - 2 Timothy 2:22

Can we in our own efforts become pure? The answer is no, but we can choose to allow Him to purify us. If we look once again at the analogy of refining gold and silver, we see that neither gold nor silver has the ability to refine itself nor to separate itself from the dross. It is only the heat of the furnace and the blowing air that removes the dross.

Are you a pure vessel for the Lord? The ultimate test that gold and silver undergo to check their purity is a testing by fire. The test is to determine its ingredients and quality.

What ingredients or attributes are inside of you? What is the quality of your life? By what standard or degree of excellence do you conduct yourself?

Gold or silver is tested by taking a sample, weighing it, then refining it and weighing it yet again. If there is no change in its weight, then all the gold is pure. If the weight changes, the gold is impure. Do you change when your situations or circumstances change in the church or in the ministry? Do you change your attitude when test and trials come?

The Bible says that God delights in a just weight. It has to do with living your life according to Godly principles. Decide today that you will live each day by the principles of God so that you will not have to continue to go around the same mountain of testing again. You don't want to be found wanting, unable to pass a test because your weights are imbalanced.

> *"Each one's work will become clear; for the Day will declare it, because it will be revealed by fire; and the fire will test each one's work, of what sort it is. If anyone's work which he has built on it endures, he will receive a reward. If anyone's work is burned, he will suffer loss; but he himself will be saved, yet so as through fire."*
> — 1 Corinthians 3:13-15

We see the concept of fire used to test and at the same time used to save.

"And I will bring the third part through the fire, and will refine them as silver is refined, and will try them as gold is tried: they shall call on my name, and I will hear them: I will say, It is my people: and they shall say, The LORD is my God."
- Zechariah 13:9

When the fire comes to test us, God shows us our own impurities. The trials reveal our weaknesses. As we persevere through the trials, we grow and overcome and become more pure. Don't run from the fire of testing. Run to it so you can dance through it and come out as a pure vessel.

We serve a God who answers by fire. Put your dance in the fire. The fire will reveal what kind of dance it is. Flesh or spirit. Put it in the fire so others can see God as you become the sights of God.

The fire belongs to the refiner. He controls the intensity of the fire. The fire separates the pure from the impure. If the dross clings to the metal, it is unusable. Let Him burn up all that is not like Him. Stay there until the purity comes.

Out of the fire, there came a sound. As Moses stood on Holy ground, the voice of God spoke to him. Moses received his mandate, his call, his purpose and his vision out of the fire. The deliverance of a nation came from the fire.

In Daniel Chapter 3, it tells us that when Shadrach, Meshach and Abednigo were in the fire, Nebuchadnezzar looked and what he saw astonished him. He didn't see the three men who had just been thrown into the fire. He saw four men in the fire, loose (free) and walking (to whirl) and the fourth looked like the Son of God.

Don't run from the fire! He is in the fire with you. You are not alone. Go deeper into the heart of God. Allow the refiner to come to your temple. Allow Him to purify you. Choose the refiner's fire.

This is the higher call.

Chapter 3

Called to Be a Vessel of Honor

God looks at all trials, both great and small, as a means to refine and test us. During the refining process, the heat of the furnace is critical. If it is too hot, the silver or gold will be vaporized and lost. If it is too cold, some of the lead will remain and the metal will not be pure.

- What vision for dance ministry has God given you?
- Are you called to go to the nations?
- Are you called to teach children to raise up the next generation?
- Are you called to use dance as evangelism?
- Are you called to have a dance studio that trains others?

   Before gold is put on the market (sent out on important assignments for the Kingdom), it has to go through a purification process. The silversmith must watch the temperature very closely to make sure that it stays exactly right. He doesn't want the vessel to be destroyed. In other words, the severity of our trials are extremely important to God. He wants us to be pure but never to be lost.

> *"For thou, O God, hast proved us: thou hast tried us, as silver is tried. Thou broughtest us into the*

net; thou laidst affliction upon our loins. Thou hast caused men to ride over our heads; we went through fire and through water: but thou broughtest us out into a wealthy place."

- Psalm 66: 10-12

As the silver or gold nears the final stage of refining, it experiences an action known as "brightening." As the last of the impurities are consumed, the now-pure molten metal suddenly emits a bright flash of light and immediately solidifies.

Take comfort in this story:

A lady went to visit a silversmith and asked to know the process of refining silver, which he fully described to her.

As she watched the silversmith, he held a piece of silver over the fire and let it heat up. He explained that in refining silver, one needed to hold the silver in the middle of the fire where the flames were hottest so as to burn away all the impurities.

The lady asked, "Sir, do you sit while the work of refining is going on?"

"Oh, yes," replied the silversmith; "I must sit with my eyes steadily fixed on the furnace, for if the time necessary for refining be exceeded in the slightest degree, the silver will be injured."

The woman was silent for a moment. Then she asked the silversmith, "How do you know when the silver is fully refined?"

He smiled at her and answered, "Oh, that's the easy part—when I see my image reflected in it."

-Author Unknown

Christ sees it as necessary to put you and I into the middle of the flames where the fire is the hottest. But His eyes are upon us. His eyes never leave us. The purpose and intent of His love for us does the work of purifying us. His wisdom and love are both engaged and intertwined in the process. Your faith will be tested! But purity comes through the refining fire.

> "Wherein ye greatly rejoice, though now for a season, if need be, ye are in heaviness through manifold temptations: That the trial of your faith, being much more precious than of gold that perisheth, though it be tried with fire, might be found unto praise and honour and glory at the appearing of Jesus Christ." - 1 Peter 1:6-7

Choose the refiner's fire. Don't resist it, refusing to hear the voice of the Refiner.

There will be a reawakening of what has been dormant in you. Fear and self-pity will vanish and will be replaced by the very image of Christ. This is the higher call.

Have we, as a corporate body of believers called to the ministry of dance, truly begun to dance... to show forth the sights of God? I ask this because in the world, dance finds its center in self. The ministry of dance must always find its center only in Christ.

Dance is a visible ministry. That's why it must flow in a pure anointing from a pure vessel. A vessel is a container or a receptacle. We must know how to possess our vessels—our bodies, properly. We must live lives of purity, holiness, honor and sanctification.

Vessels, especially vases, are defined as having a certain anatomy. The lowest part is the foot, a distinguishable base to the piece. Are you careful about where your feet go? Are you allowing the Lord to order your steps or are your feet quick in running to do that which is out of the will of God?

> "These six things doth the LORD hate: yea, seven are an abomination unto him: A proud look, a lying tongue, and hands that shed innocent blood, An heart that deviseth wicked imaginations, feet that be swift in running to mischief, A false witness that speaketh lies, and he that soweth discord among brethren."
>
> - Proverbs 6:16-19

Next is the body, which forms the main portion of the piece. Resting atop the body is the shoulder, where the body curves inward. In the Old Testament, the priest carried the ark on their shoulders. The shoulders represent how we carry things. The ark represented the presence of God. Are you daily shouldering or carrying the presence of the Lord everywhere you go? His presence rests upon your shoulders.

The neck gives the vessel more height. Make sure you are not a stiff-necked person, someone whose behavior is haughty or stubborn.

> *"Now be ye not stiffnecked, as your fathers were, but yield yourselves unto the LORD, and enter into his sanctuary, which he hath sanctified for ever: and serve the LORD your God, that the fierceness of his wrath may turn away from you."*
> - 2 Chronicles 30:8

The design of the base may have in many shapes. It can be found, flat, or a variety of other shapes. But it is still a vessel that can be used.

> *"I will praise thee; for I am fearfully and wonderfully made: marvellous are thy works; and that my soul knoweth right well."* - Psalm 139:14

Lastly, the lip, where the vase flares back out at the top. When a potter makes a vase, the lip of it has to be exactly right in order for it to pour correctly. Otherwise, the potter will take the vase and throw it back on the wheel and break it, then remake it again so that the lip can be formed properly.

- What words are coming out of your mouth?

- Do you speak words that are edifying to the listener?

- Are the words of your mouth acceptable in His sight?

- Are you a vessel that is ready for the Master to use?

> *"Nevertheless the foundation of God standeth sure, having this seal, The Lord knoweth them that are his. And, Let every one that nameth the name of Christ depart from iniquity. But in a great house there are not only vessels of gold and of silver, but also of wood and of earth; and some to honour, and some to dishonour. If a man therefore purge himself from these, he shall be a vessel unto honour, sanctified, and meet for the master's use, and prepared unto every good work. Flee also youthful lusts: but follow righteousness, faith, charity, peace, with them that call on the Lord out of a pure heart."*
> — 2 Timothy 2:19-22

- Will you show forth dances of gold that shine bright because they are born from a pure, surrendered life?

- Will your dances be dances of silver?

Silver is sometimes seen as less desirable than gold, but silver has special properties. Pure silver is the best conductor of heat and electricity. It's considered to be the best reflector of visible light, which is why it is commonly used to make mirrors. Does your life reflect Jesus Christ? Is He seen when people see you? Do you reflect Him as if looking into a mirror?

Silver does tarnish and turn dark grey when exposed to air, requiring periodic polishing. Each day, you are exposed to that which life brings, whether it's good "air quality" or bad. Air quality is determined by the condition of the air around us. Good air quality refers to clean, clear, unpolluted air.

Clean air is essential to maintaining the delicate balance of life. Poor air quality occurs when pollutants reach high enough concentrations to severely affect our health and/or our environment. Our daily choices can have a significant impact on our spiritual air quality. Therefore, we must allow Holy Spirit to daily polish our hearts with the Word of God.

- Will your dances be wood and earth?

Wood and earth speak of the fragility of our humanity. It speaks of lives that are dry, sensual, carnal and worldly—lives of those who mind earth and earthly things. We can never lean to the arm of flesh or to our own understanding.

CALLED TO BE A VESSEL OF HONOR

- Will your life be for honor or dishonor?

> *"If a man therefore purge himself from these, he shall be a vessel unto honour, sanctified, and meet for the master's use, and prepared unto every good work. Flee also youthful lusts: but follow righteousness, faith, charity, peace, with them that call on the Lord out of a pure heart."*
>
> - 2 Timothy 2:21-22

Depart from all iniquity. Thoroughly cleanse yourself. Call on the Lord with a pure heart, without mixture or wrong motives.

This is the higher call.

Chapter 4

Called to Be a True Worshiper

The first time we see the word "dance" mentioned in the Bible is found in the book of Exodus:

> *"And Miriam the prophetess, the sister of Aaron, took a timbrel in her hand; and all the women went out after her with timbrels and with dances."* - Exodus 15:20

The children of Israel had been in bondage to Pharaoh for hundreds of years. When they cried out to Him for a deliverer, God sent Moses. God brought them through the Red Sea, which represents the blood of Jesus. It speaks to the fact that we have been delivered from sin, death, hell and the grave itself.

It then tells us that Miriam led all of the women in dance. In fact, it shows us that she sang while she danced, while she played her instrument.

It's very significant that she was the one who led them. It was a custom in those days for the closest female relative to go out and meet or greet the returning victor after they had won a battle. Moses was the victor and Miriam was his closest female relative. Jesus is our Victor and we are His betrothed, His closest female relative.

The closer His return gets, the more you will see an increase in dancing. Even as their dances showed forth

God's victory, our dances must also show forth the victories of our God.

Notice that they danced after they were delivered, not while they were still in bondage. Deliverance will release a dance of victory that's not possible while you are still in bondage to the world, your flesh or the devil. Check your movements. They speak to the degree of your freedom and deliverance.

There is no scripture in the Word of God that mentions sitting and watching dance, other than when King Herod was enticed by watching Salome.

> "And when the daughter of the said Herodias came in, and danced, and pleased Herod and them that sat with him, the king said unto the damsel, Ask of me whatsoever thou wilt, and I will give it thee. And he sware unto her, Whatsoever thou shalt ask of me, I will give it thee, unto the half of my kingdom. And she went forth, and said unto her mother, What shall I ask? And she said, The head of John the Baptist." - Mark 6:22-24

Although her name means peace, her life produced just the opposite. Beware of being influenced by others, even those closest to us. Carry out fully the divine intent and purpose for your ministry so as not to misuse your gift in any way.

DANCE: THE HIGHER CALL

2 Timothy 4:5 is translated this way in the New International Version: *"But you, keep your head in all situations... discharge all the duties of your ministry."* Keep your head in all situations so no one else will lose theirs.

Throughout the scriptures, dance was meant to be congregational. We see this clearly in the Psalms.

> *"Let them praise his name in the dance: let them sing praises unto him with the timbrel and harp."*
> - Psalm 149:3

> *"Praise him with the timbrel and dance: praise him with stringed instruments and organs."*
> - Psalm 150:4

The word "let" means it's ok! You have permission! The word "them" means everyone! Men, women, boys and girls.

"Praise" is the Hebrew word halal. Strong's Concordance defines it this way: to be clear (orig. of sound, but usually of color); to shine; hence, to make a show, to boast; and thus to be (clamorously) foolish; to rave; causatively, to celebrate; also to stultify:--(make) boast (self), celebrate, commend, (deal, make), fool(-ish, -ly), glory, give (light), be (make, feign self) mad (against), give in marriage, (sing, be worthy of) praise, rage, renowned, shine. His name is His honor, His character and His authority.

The word "dance" is the word machowl, which is a round, circle dance. It comes from the word chuwl, which according to Strong's Concordance, means chiyl {kheel}; to twist or whirl (in a circular or spiral manner), i.e. (specifically) to dance, to writhe in pain (especially of parturition) or fear; figuratively, to wait, to pervert:--bear, (make to) bring forth, (make to) calve, dance, drive away, fall grievously (with pain), fear, form, great, grieve, (be) grievous, hope, look, make, be in pain, be much (sore) pained, rest, shake, shapen, (be) sorrow(-ful), stay, tarry, travail (with pain), tremble, trust, wait carefully (patiently), be wounded.

They danced when they came together as a corporate, collective people to celebrate His name, His honor, His character and His authority. Let your life be a dance that all can see—a life that reflects and celebrates His name, His honor, His character and His authority.

To function as a minister of dance, there is something we must understand. The first responsibility is to minister to God. The priests of the Old Testament would go to God and minister to Him on behalf of the people. Only after going to God, could they minister to the people for God on behalf of God. Priests had to be physically whole as well as holy in their conduct. It is crucial for us to have a hidden place in God if we are called to public ministry.

"Blessed is the man that heareth me, watching daily at my gates, waiting at the posts of my doors. For whoso findeth me findeth life, and shall obtain favour of the LORD."

- Proverbs 8:34-35

Happy is the man who hears daily. To hear means to come under what you have heard and walk in obedience to it. If you will make that your guide, you will dance His dances, not your own.

It is necessary that we hear Him. We must be clear in what we are communicating so as not to confuse the people with messages that are not from God. The Bible does not say that God seeks dancers. It says God seeks those who will worship Him.

"But the hour cometh, and now is, when the true worshippers shall worship the Father in spirit and in truth: for the Father seeketh such to worship him. God is a Spirit: and they that worship him must worship him in spirit and in truth."

- John 4:23-24

When we talk about the ministry of dance, we often hear people say he or she was anointed. What does that mean? Do we know the difference between when someone is anointed and when someone has a gift?

To anoint means to smear with oil. If I ask you right now, "Do you want the anointing?" I'm sure you will shout, "yes!"

Read the story below:

Matthew 26:6-16

6 *Now when Jesus was in Bethany, in the house of Simon the leper,*

7 *There came unto him a woman having an alabaster box of very precious ointment, and poured it on his head, as he sat at meat.*

8 *But when his disciples saw it, they had indignation, saying, To what purpose is this waste?*

9 *For this ointment might have been sold for much, and given to the poor.*

10 *When Jesus understood it, he said unto them, Why trouble ye the woman? for she hath wrought a good work upon me.*

11 *For ye have the poor always with you; but me ye have not always.*

12 *For in that she hath poured this ointment on my body, she did it for my burial.*

13 *Verily I say unto you, Wheresoever this gospel shall be preached in the whole world, there shall also this, that this woman hath done, be told for a memorial of her.*

14 *Then one of the twelve, called Judas Iscariot, went unto the chief priests,*

15 *And said unto them, What will ye give me, and I will deliver him unto you? And they covenanted with him for thirty pieces of silver.*

16 *And from that time he sought opportunity to betray him.*

The woman with the alabaster box came to Jesus. The Bible describes it as being filled with precious ointment. It must have been very costly because as she poured it on Jesus, those sitting in the room said it could have been sold and the money could've been used for the poor.

Notice the response of Jesus. He said that she had anointed Him for His burial. Part of their cultural preparation for burial included anointing human remains with sweet-smelling oils in devotion as well for the practical intent of obscuring the stench of death.

When God releases His anointing upon our lives, it is for our burial so that we can live resurrected lives. Our dances must be dances of resurrection life so we can release the fragrance of Christ without the stench of death that the self life brings.

> *"Now thanks be unto God, which always causeth us to triumph in Christ, and maketh manifest the savour of his knowledge by us in every place. For we are unto God a sweet savour of Christ, in them that are saved, and in them that perish."*
> — 2 Corinthians 2:14-15

You will notice in the story that as soon as Jesus was anointed for his burial, Judas went and saw an opportunity to betray him. When God anoints you and you surrender to the anointing in such a way that the savor of Christ is released, you can rest assure that the enemy will rise up against you.

Don't be surprised if those who should be there to walk with you, seek an opportunity to betray you. Don't take it personally. It is because of the anointing. You're in good company.

More important than recognizing the anointing is knowing the One who gives the anointing—Christ, the anointed One. The Lord is looking for a pure, spotless bride. One with singleness of vision, one who has doves eyes—one who sees only Him. He is looking for the one who desires only Him. He is looking for the one who will lay down their life for His. That's the person upon whom He will place His anointing.

The anointing was only placed upon consecrated objects, those things that had been set aside for Holy use. Are your eyes set aside for Him? Are you careful what you allow into your eye gates?

Are your words set aside for Him? Are they edifying to the listener? Do you avoid gossip? Is your time consecrated for His use? Have you truly consecrated your life fully?

Go beyond the dance to the Lord of the dance. Live a fully consecrated life without compromise. When He comes to inquire, will He find a true worshiper in you? There is no true worship without obedience.

This is the higher call.

Chapter 5

Called to Live a Life of Complete Obedience

The first mention of worship is found in Genesis 22. God gave instructions to Abraham to take his son Issac and offer him as a sacrifice.

> *"And he said, Take now thy son, thine only son Isaac, whom thou lovest, and get thee into the land of Moriah; and offer him there for a burnt offering upon one of the mountains which I will tell thee of. And Abraham rose up early in the morning, and saddled his ass, and took two of his young men with him, and Isaac his son, and clave the wood for the burnt offering, and rose up, and went unto the place of which God had old him. Then on the third day Abraham lifted up his eyes, and saw the place afar off. And Abraham said unto his young men, Abide ye here with the ass; and I and the lad will go yonder and worship, and come again to you."*
> - Genesis 22:2-5

Abraham said to his servants that he and Issac were going to worship. Notice, neither Abraham not Issac had any of the things we associate with worship. They had no CD, no CD player, no iPad, no iPod, no cell phone with their favorite music, no worship team, no choir. How would they worship?

Abraham would offer to God that which was most precious to him, his son Isaac. But Isaac was not what really what God was after. God wanted His heart. It was a test of his faith and love for God. Abraham passed the test. Pure worship manifests in obedience.

When he was about to slay his son, an angel called out to him.

> "And Abraham stretched forth his hand, and took the knife to slay his son. And the angel of the LORD called unto him out of heaven, and said, Abraham, Abraham: and he said, Here am I. And he said, Lay not thine hand upon the lad, neither do thou any thing unto him: for now I know that thou fearest God, seeing thou hast not withheld thy son, thine only son from me. A nd Abraham lifted up his eyes, and looked, and behold behind him a ram caught in a thicket by his horns: and Abraham went and took the ram, and offered him up for a burnt offering in the stead of his son. And Abraham called the name of that place Jehovah Jireh: as it is said to this day, In the mount of the LORD it shall be seen."
>
> - Genesis 22:10-14

Abraham said, "Here am I." Here am I is the Hebrew word, HINENI. It is not the same as "Here I am." HINENI is a bottom line statement: Lord, Here am I. My mind. My body. My soul. My spirit.

It is an unequivocal acceptance of whatever God asks of you. The ministry of dance will require all of you. You will have plenty of opportunities to live a life of HINENI through your obedience to the overall vision of the ministry of your church, your dance leader or your pastor.

When God is asking us to do something important or critical to the expansion of His Kingdom, HINENI is the response God is looking for. Abraham is known as a surrendered, obedient worshiper of God. What will history say about you?

We are all called to something pivotal in the plan of God. When you say Here am I (HINENI) to God, you enter into a place of total dedication and obedience to the covenant. HINENI is absolute submission to the sovereignty of God. Here am I completely, totally—my spirit, my soul, my mind, my will, my emotions, my body—every part of me is yours.

HINENI is saying "Yes" to God from the deepest parts of who you are. God is not just calling you to dance ministry. He is calling you to a place called HINENI.

HINENI says to God, no matter what, here I stand. I draw the line and I will not turn back. I'm not moving. Here I am to worship. I'm not moving and you cannot back me up.

There is a price that comes with standing that has to do with you and the Creator—not your ministry, not your affiliation—HINENI acknowledges His absolute sovereignty in your life. Creation is waiting for the manifestation of the sons of God and we are called to this place called Hineni, not for our own benefit but to acknowledge His glory in the earth.

HINENI is identifying with the cross of Christ. Through Jesus, God's love came through time and space in the person of Jesus Christ. God revealed His heart to us as He gave His only begotten Son for us.

His sacrifice was the fulfillment of what God began with Abraham when he went up on the mountain to worship. It was the Genesis of the cross. God spared Isaac, yet He Himself completed the sacrifice and gave His only begotten Son.

When Jesus laid down His life, it was an act of worship to the Father. His HINENI took Him to a place of obedience, even death on a cross. Jesus is the HINENI of God revealed to mankind. Jesus said YES to the will of the Father.

> *"And Abraham lifted up his eyes, and looked, and behold behind him a ram caught in a thicket by his horns: and Abraham went and took the ram, and offered him up for a burnt offering in the stead of his son."* - Genesis 22:13

When Abraham lifted up his eyes, God said, "I see."

"And Abraham called the name of that place Jehovahjireh: as it is said to this day, In the mount of the LORD it shall be seen."

- Genesis 22:14

Jehovah Jireh means the Lord will see to it. When a God hears your HINENI, He will see to your situation. He cares about all things that concern you.

HINENI is the highest form of worship. We say HINENI with our lives. The disciples said HINENI with their lives. Our Hineni can change nations.

The Bible is filled with stories of those worshipers who won the heart of the King with their HINENI. HINENI is being willing to do what no one else can do. The Bible is filled with those who said HINENI!

- The HINENI of Esther saved a nation.

- The HINENI of David killed a giant.

- The HINENI of Nehemiah rebuilt the walls.

- The HINENI of Moses delivered a nation.

It is time for you to write your own story. Will your HINENI:

- Make you a father of many nations? (Abraham)

- Kill a giant and make you a king? (David)

- Send you with the Word of God in your mouth to speak to nations? (Isaiah)

- Save a nation? (Esther)

- Rebuild walls of broken lives? (Nehemiah)

Will you say yes to His call? Some of us cannot even say yes to getting to rehearsal on time or walk in agreement with our dance leader. We always have an opinion about everything instead of seeking God for His opinion.

Some of us are saying yes to ungodly attitudes, unforgiveness, fear, sowing discord among each other or jealousy. You must say HINENI every day. Common people do occasionally what uncommon people do daily. Be uncommon. Your HINENI can change the world. Full surrender, complete obedience. This is the higher call.

Live a life of unrestrained worship. David was a man after God's heart. He first set worship in order when he established the tabernacle of worship.

After David captured Jerusalem from the Jebusites, one of his first acts was to bring the Ark of the Covenant, representing the Presence of God into Jerusalem, and establish worshipers continually, ministering to the Lord day and night.

When the tabernacle of David was established, David unveiled an aspect of worship that had never been known. He was known as the undignified worshiper because it was said that it was certainly un-

dignified for a king to display himself in such a manner
as he danced before His God.

> *"And Michal the daughter of Saul came out to
> meet David, and said, How glorious was the king
> of Israel today, who uncovered himself today in
> the eyes of the handmaids of his servants, as one
> of the vain fellows shamelessly uncovereth him-
> self! And David said unto Michal, It was before
> the LORD, which chose me before thy father,
> and before all his house, to appoint me ruler
> over the people of the LORD, over Israel:
> therefore will I play before the LORD. And I will
> yet be more vile than thus, and will be base in
> mine own sight: and of themaidservants which
> thou hast spoken of, of them shall I be had in
> honour."* - 2 Samuel 6:20-22

David was leaping and stamping wildly for joy as if the
limbs of his body would come off. He did not care who
was looking. His only concern was to please the heart
of the King.

What started in his spirit was experienced in his soul
and expressed in his physical body. As David acted fully
in accordance to God's will, he was fulfilling what was in
God's heart. He was obedient. Because David was a
man after God's heart, David unlocked that which no
one else had unlocked. As a result, the worship of
heaven was released in his tabernacle.

Twice in the Word of God, in Isaiah and in Revelation, it mentions the key of David. The ability of this key was to open what no man could shut and shut things no man could open. It represents having legitimate authority to rule. This key was specifically called the key of David.

Why is it called the Key "of David?" Why is David's name associated with this Key of Governmental Authority, the key that has the power to open what no one can shut and shut what no one can open? I believe that the answer is found in what the Lord Himself says concerning David:

> "I have found David the son of Jesse, a man after mine own heart, which shall fulfil all my will."
>
> - Acts 13:22

I believe the Key of David is essentially the heart of David. God calls him "a man after My own heart."

One writer wrote about this passage of Scripture: "God did not say I found David to be a great warrior, or a brilliant king. He said, I found David to care about the things I care about. David was a man whose heartbeat was in sync with mine. When I look right, David looked right. When I looked left, David looked left. When I said I care about something, David said, I care about that too." That is what it means to be a man after God's own heart.

The heart of David can best be seen in these words:

> *"How he sware unto the LORD, and vowed unto the mighty God of Jacob; Surely I will not come into the tabernacle of my house, nor go up into my bed; I will not give sleep to mine eyes, or slumber to mine eyelids, Until I find out a place for the LORD, an habitation for the mighty God of Jacob."* - Psalm 132:2-5

David made a vow and devoted his life to finding a resting place, a dwelling place for God. David vowed to live in extravagant worship to the Lord. He said YES with all of his resources, time, talents, treasures.

According to Psalm 132, the heart of David, above all, was to find a resting place for the presence of the Lord among His people, a "dwelling for the Mighty One of Jacob." David was known as a shepherd, a fugitive, a warrior, and a king; but most of all, and above all, as a worshiper.

David was a man after God's own heart. God's heart, above all, is to be in the midst of His people. This is the dominant theme of Scriptures, from Genesis where God walked with mankind in the cool of the Garden, to Revelation where we hear a "loud voice from the throne" saying "NOW (finally ... again!) the dwelling of God is with men, and He will live with them." This is the purpose and heart of God; that is where history is heading and our ultimate destiny; that is why Jesus came as Immanuel, God with us, to reconcile all things to the Father.

It is to those whose hearts line up with God's heart that God is prepared to entrust the Key of David. These are the ones to whom He wishes to impart the same authority that David walked in, to open doors that no one can shut, and shut doors that no one can open.

Let's look at the life of David. God called him at age 13. Was he king the next day? No! He was faithfully shepherding his father's sheep. It was 17 years until he saw even a partial fulfillment of the prophecy that he received when Samuel anointed him and laid hands on him. It was a process from the time he was anointed to be king to the time he was actually crowned as king.

- David remained faithful. David stayed true to God while serving Saul. HINENI.

- He was faithful during his times of testing. He was on the run because Saul was jealous and tried to kill him. His destiny was to rule. HINENI.

- His destiny was to be king of all of Israel. Do not give up on the way to your destiny. HINENI.

Maintain your integrity. Remain steadfast. Don't waver in your faith. Don't lose heart. Do not become weary. Keep a good attitude during your process. HINENI!

Do not blame the enemy when a situation or circumstance is part of your destiny. David loved and served Saul, but righteous acts are not always rewarded.

Because of His HINENI, ultimately, his destiny brought him into the place of rulership. He could have become bitter, blaming God or the devil for his circumstances while he was running and hiding in caves. He could have murmured or complained or allowed discouragement to set in. Yet, he remained faithful to God. Even Jesus had a garden process to go through to reach the cross, the resurrection, and ultimately, the throne.

Your prophetic destiny is real. It's wonderful. It's God-ordained. It's exciting. If you encounter challenges along the way, it will be worth it all. HINENI!

David was an unquenchable worshiper who lived in a world filled with many things that could have taken his attention away from the King. The unquenchable worshiper is different. No matter what competes for their attention in this world, they maintain a heart that burns with a love that cannot be extinguished. No matter what, they will not allow that love to be quenched.

"Set me as a seal upon thine heart, as a seal upon thine arm: for love is strong as death; jealousy is cruel as the grave: the coals thereof

are coals of fire, which hath a most vehement flame." - Song of Solomon 8:6

The HINENI of David rang loud in the heart of God. His unquenchable worship released a HINENI that killed a giant. He was willing to do what no one else was willing to do, or at times, able to do. I believe that we too can be a people after God's own heart.

To the obedient, unquenchable worshiper, He releases new vision to see. To the obedient, unquenchable worshiper, He releases an anointing that opens the ears to hear. The more we see, the more we hear, the more we worship... the more we want to walk in obedience to our King. Live a life of unrestrained worship.

This is the higher call.

Chapter 6
Called to Live a Life of Sacrifice

Isaiah was an undone worshiper.

> *"In the year that king Uzziah died I saw also the Lord sitting upon a throne, high and lifted up, and his train filled the temple. Above it stood the seraphims: each one had six wings; with twain he covered his face, and with twain he covered his feet, and with twain he did fly. And one cried unto another, and said, Holy, holy, holy, is the LORD of hosts: the whole earth is full of his glory. And the posts of the door moved at the voice of him that cried, and the house was filled with smoke. Then said I, Woe is me! for I am undone; because I am a man of unclean lips, and I dwell in the midst of a people of unclean lips: f or mine eyes have seen the King, the LORD of hosts."* - Isaiah 6:1-5

The word "undone" is defined as destroyed. When the grandeur and glory of the Lord was revealed, the prophet declared his own destroyed condition in the light of eternal perfection. In the presence of our King, our old self dies and in His unfailing, unfathomable, undeniable love, He meets us.

"Then flew one of the seraphims unto me, having a live coal in his hand, which he had taken with the tongs from off the altar: And he laid it upon my mouth, and said, Lo, this hath touched thy lips; and thine iniquity is taken away, and thy sin purged. Also I heard the voice of the Lord, saying, Whom shall I send, and who will go for us? Then said I, Here am I; send me."

- Isaiah 6:6-8

The call comes to each of us—the call to sacrificial worship and service that pleases the heart of the King and shows forth His glory. The prophet Isaiah said, "Here am I." He was saying HINENI, HINENI, HINENI.

"And he said, Go, and tell this people, Hear ye indeed, but understand not; and see ye indeed, but perceive not. Make the heart of this people fat, and make their ears heavy, and shut their eyes; lest they see with their eyes, and hear with their ears, and understand with their heart, and convert, and be healed." - Isaiah 6:9-10

Your HINENI might make you unpopular. Once you fully surrender to the fire and determine to reveal Christ, you step into a realm with God that others may not understand. The revealing of Christ is worth the death to self. Be the sight of a nation saved.

CALLED TO LIVE A LIFE OF SACRIFICE

There was a HINENI that was born from a heart of worship that won the heart of the king. God was revealed through Esther in such a powerful way that it saved a nation. She was a sacrificial worshiper. Her willingness to sacrifice her own life to save her people was the ultimate essence of worship.

Esther's story is not one we usually look to for insights about worship because we don't see the word worship. We tend to look on the surface or for things that are familiar. Before she became queen, Esther was just a girl, reverent before God and a servant of her people.

In her humility, she was lifted to significance for a divine purpose. As we take a closer look at Esther's story, we find she demonstrates a characteristic of a true obedient worshiper—quiet submission. She was a faithful worshiper. And, in turn, we see that God's faithfulness to her was His answer to her HINENI.

> "And the king loved Esther above all the women, and she obtained grace and favour in his sight more than all the virgins; so that he set the royal crown upon her head, and made her queen..."
>
> - Esther 2:17

Esther had won his heart. He was prepared to give her up to half of his kingdom if that had been her request. The king extended the scepter to her. The plot against God's people was revealed and the enemy was destroyed. When you have won the heart of the King, He will make sure that the plans of the enemy against you are revealed and uncovered.

Jesus is our Golden Scepter. We can go boldly before God's throne and claim victory over every spirit of Haman that tries to come against us. When God hears your HINENI—when He hears your yes to His call, you can rest assured that no weapon formed against you will prosper. Not only was Haman destroyed, so were his 10 sons. Every assignment of the enemy will come to nothing.

> *"For if thou altogether holdest thy peace at this time, then shall there enlargement and deliverance arise to the Jews from another place; but thou and thy father's house shall be destroyed: and who knoweth whether thou art come to the kingdom for such a time as this?"*
>
> - Esther 4:14

Esther's name means star. Each of us is called to shine bright like the stars to reflect the glory of God. Each star is different in color.

The difference in colors actually depends on many different factors. The first is the composition of a star. While stars are all basically composed of atoms some stars have other trace elements in them that can alter the wavelengths of light that they emit. That's why purity is so important. We want His light within us to shine as bright as possible without any elements of this world to distort the clarity.

The next factor is its surface temperature. This is the most significant contributor to a star's color. The change in temperature changes the wavelength of light a star emits. The fire that the refiner uses must be hot in order to bring us to a place of brightness for others to see.

Have you ever seen an open flame? A blue flame is a flame burning at very high temperatures. Yellow flames have temperatures that are cooler than blue flames and red flames are the coolest of them all. The same thing happens with stars. Very hot stars tend to be blue stars. Stars with an average surface temperature become yellow stars like our sun. At what temperature are you burning to reflect His image?

Depending on the kind of light an element burns, scientists can analyze a star's light and basically determine its elemental composition. People can see and determine what's inside of you depending on what kind of light you emit.

This is not the time for you to hold your peace. This is the time for you to shine and emit the light of God. God who is Light has placed a spirit within you. You decide who you will become. Don't let anyone else dance for you. Don't let anyone else worship for you or preach for you. Don't let anyone else do what you know God has called you to do. Don't compare yourself to anyone else. You shine bright!

Will you be a temple who displays the glory of the King? Esther said, "If I perish, I perish." Is that your answer? Are you prepared to give all?

- Esther took the kingdom by force!

- She knew she was royalty, chosen to be a solution for her people.

- She took control of the destiny of her people.

- She knew she was destined to change history!

- She dealt with the spirit of Haman, he and his sons.

Every spirit attached to the assignment of the enemy was overthrown by her determination, passion and strategies of wisdom. You have been called, given a destiny and ultimately set free to change history and reveal the risen Christ. Someone in this generation is going to make a noise that's going to shake a nation. Why not you?

Nehemiah was an authentic, obedient worshipper, unafraid to serve God in the midst of opposition and ridicule. As Nehemiah served in a high government position as cup bearer to the king, his friends came to him with news from home. Nehemiah then had a choice. Was he to only have sympathy for the situation or was God calling him to act? He chose to be a solution for his nation.

CALLED TO LIVE A LIFE OF SACRIFICE

Let's take a close look at the words of Nehemiah:

"The words of Nehemiah the son of Hachaliah. And it came to pass in the month Chisleu, in the twentieth year, as I was in Shushan the palace, That Hanani, one of my brethren, came, he and certain men of Judah; and I asked them concerning the Jews that had escaped, which were left of the captivity, and concerning Jerusalem. And they said unto me, The remnant that are left of the captivity there in the province are in great affliction and reproach: the wall of Jerusalem also is broken down, and the gates thereof are burned with fire. And it came to pass, when I heard these words, that I sat down and wept, and mourned certain days, and fasted, and prayed before the God of heaven."
— Nehemiah 1:1-4

Look at the response of Nehemiah. He wept. He mourned. He fasted and prayed.

Nehemiah begins with worship, focusing on God's character, acknowledging to God that He is great, awesome and a God of love. He is the God of wonders beyond our galaxy. He is Lord of heaven and earth. Unto Him belongs all glory, honor and praise.

We can imagine how Nehemiah must have meditated on all the ways to worship God by lifting his name on high. There was no music and no worship leader. He simply meditated on and declared the truths of God.

Then, Nehemiah focuses on God, acknowledging God's power and majesty. He began to confess sin. While worshiping God, He saw God's holiness. You cannot spend time in authentic worship without humbling yourself before God.

Nehemiah confessed before God that their nation had forgotten the words that God had spoken. He openly acknowledged that his heart, his father's house, and his nation had grown dim. He focused on God's Justice.

> *"And said, I beseech thee, O LORD God of heaven, the great and terrible God, that keepeth covenant and mercy for them that love him and observe his commandments: Let thine ear now be attentive, and thine eyes open, that thou mayest hear the prayer of thy servant, which I pray before thee now, day and night, for the children of Israel thy servants, and confess the sins of the children of Israel, which we have sinned against thee: both I and my father's house have sinned. We have dealt very corruptly against thee, and have not kept the commandments, nor the statutes, nor the judgments, which thou commandedst thy servant Moses."*
>
> - Nehemiah 1:5-7

CALLED TO LIVE A LIFE OF SACRIFICE

And then his request came to God as He put God in remembrance of His Word to His people:

> *"Remember, I beseech thee, the word that thou commandedst thy servant Moses, saying, If ye transgress, I will scatter you abroad among the nations: But if ye turn unto me, and keep my commandments, and do them; though there were of you cast out unto the uttermost part of the heaven, yet will I gather them from thence, and will bring them unto the place that I have chosen to set my name there. Now these are thy servants and thy people, whom thou hast redeemed by thy great power, and by thy strong hand. O Lord, I beseech thee, let now thine ear be attentive to the prayer of thy servant, and to the prayer of thy servants, who desire to fear thy name: and prosper, I pray thee, thy servant this day, and grant him mercy in the sight of this man. For I was the king's cupbearer."*
> - Nehemiah 1:8-11

Because he had won the heart of the king that he served, he found favor and God sent him to rebuild the walls. In fact, the king provided all that he needed to rebuild the walls.

God is calling for us, the authentic worshipers, to say HINENI. Here am I. I will go to rebuild the walls of human heart, rebuild the walls of our communities.

Worship will lift the reproach. We will worship, we will watch, we will war. HINENI.

We will go to the gates of education, government or entertainment—whatever sphere of authority the King gives us. Our lives must become the living, walking tabernacle carrying the glory, the presence of the Lord.

- Where are the sons of God?

- Where are the obedient, unquenchable worshipers whose hearts are fixed on the King?

- Where are the unstoppable worshipers?

- Where are the obedient, undone, authentic worshipers?

David, Esther, Nehemiah—they each had to lay down their lives for the purposes of God. The world is waiting for the sons of God. They are not waiting for YOU but for the Spirit of God in you.

The old man must die. You cannot put the new man, made in the image of Christ, on top of the old man of flesh. You must completely take the old man off. The flesh nature must be considered dead so the new man can truly live. Dances of resurrection life will not come forth unless you mortify—put to death, your flesh.

"If so be that ye have heard him, and have been taught by him, as the truth is in Jesus: That ye put off concerning the former conversation the

old man, which is corrupt according to the deceitful lusts; And be renewed in the spirit of your mind; And that ye put on the new man, which after God is created in righteousness and true holiness." - Ephesians 4:21-24

"Mortify therefore your members which are up-on the earth; fornication, uncleanness, inordinate affection, evil concupiscence, and covetousness, which is idolatry: For which things' sake the wrath of God cometh on the children of dis-obedience: In the which ye also walked some time, when ye lived in them. But now ye also put off all these; anger, wrath, malice, blasphemy, filthy communication out of your mouth. Lie not one to another, seeing that ye have put off the old man with his deeds; And have put on the new man, which is renewed in knowledge after the image of him that created him."
- Colossians 3:5-10

"Therefore, brethren, we are debtors, not to the flesh, to live after the flesh. For if ye live after the flesh, ye shall die: but if ye through the Spirit do mortify the deeds of the body, ye shall live. For as many as are led by the Spirit of God, they are the sons of God." - Romans 8:12-14

Are your dances flesh or spirit? Whether we realize it or not, many people often dance to touch emotions instead of ministering through Holy Spirit. Is your life lived in the flesh or in the spirit? Do you allow Holy Spirit to lead you each day?

Our ordinary gifts and abilities will never worship God unless they are transformed by Holy Spirit living in us, ruling and reigning in our hearts, thoughts and words. Only then can we live and dance for His purpose.

This is the higher call.

Chapter 7

Called to Worship in Truth

The message of worshiping the Lord "in spirit and truth" comes from Jesus' conversation with the woman at the well in John 4:6-30. In the conversation, the woman was discussing places of worship with Jesus, saying that the Jews worshiped at Jerusalem, while the Samaritans worshiped at Mount Gerizim.

Jesus had just revealed that He knew about her many husbands, as well as the fact that the current man she lived with was not her husband. This made her uncomfortable, so she attempted to divert His attention from her personal life to matters of religion.

Jesus refused to be distracted from His lesson on true worship and got to the heart of the matter: "But the hour is coming, and now is, when the true worshipers shall worship the Father in spirit and truth, for the Father seeks such to worship Him (John 4:23).

The overall lesson about worshiping the Lord in spirit and truth is that worship of God is not to be confined to a single geographical location. Worship is a matter of the heart, not external actions. Worship is rooted and directed by truth rather than by tradition.

In Deuteronomy 6:4, Moses told the Israelites how they were to love their God: "You shall love the Lord your God with all your heart and with all your soul and with all your might." Our worship of God is directed by our love for Him; as we love, we worship. The idea of "might" in Hebrew indicates totality, but Jesus expanded this expression to "mind" and "strength." To worship God in spirit and truth involves loving Him with heart, soul, mind and strength.

Spirit without truth leads to error, false religions and deception. Truth without spirit can result in a dry, passionless encounter that can easily lead to a form of joyless legalism.

> *"Then said Jesus to those Jews which believed on him, If ye continue in my word, then are ye my disciples indeed; And ye shall know the truth, and the truth shall make you free."*
>
> *- John 8:31-32*

We understand from reading this passage that truth leads to freedom. Truth is that which is not concealed. The enemy hides in darkness. It's not always easy to face truth but is necessary.

> *"Behold, thou desirest truth in the inward parts."*
>
> *- Psalm 51:6*

What is truth? Truth is defined as that which is in accordance with facts or reality. So truth is reality.

We cannot have our own version of "truth" if it is not God's truth. If we do, we will not be free. But the

58

truth is that there is only one real truth. Truth is a person and His name is Jesus.

In John 14:6, Jesus said, "I am the way, the truth and the life." There are dancers who have their own versions of what they have come to believe is their truth. Meet 6 of them:

1. "Wanda World" likes to keep up with the Joneses and wear the latest clothes. She just wants to look good when she dances. She spends her time on Facebook day and night so she doesn't miss the latest happenings.

2. "Fanny Flesh" sleeps with her boyfriend. They live together. She thinks they will get married. She thinks she will get him saved. Although her pastor has told her that living together before marriage is wrong, her favorite saying is, "God knows my heart."

3. "Tammy Technique" is only concerned about having the best technique. As long as her leaps, turns, tendus and double pirouettes are better than everyone else's, she happy. She believes that beginners have no right to be in dance ministry. Instead of helping them, she looks down on "poor beginners."

4. "Heavenly Helen" is just "no earthly good." During every rehearsal, she can't focus because she's speaking in tongues and receiving revelation from heaven. She

never helps with anything. She just wants to pray and she wants everybody else to pray. She thinks it's her job to correct everybody.

5. "Felicia Fear" is afraid of everything. She's afraid to dance. When she does dance, she's afraid to be in front for fear somebody might see her. She's afraid to speak out loud; afraid to lead in any capacity. She's even afraid to be set free.

6. "Ida I Don't Know" lacks focus and awareness. Just ask Ida, "What time are we scheduled to minister?" Her response, "I don't know." Ask Ida, "What garment are we wearing Sunday?" Her response: "I don't know."

7. "Noelle Know-It-All" thinks she is God's gift to dance ministry. She easily criticizes what she thinks are the faults and shortcomings of others. She thinks she knows it all so she doesn't hesitate to correct everybody.

8. "Isabelle Intimidated" puts on a brave face as the dance leader. She's stays within the four walls of her church even though she has been invited to go to seminars and conferences so she can go higher—thus taking the ministry and those in the dance ministry to a new level. She won't go and she doesn't want the team members to go. She says she is being "faithful to the house." The truth is, she's intimidated whenever she

thinks of going outside of her comfort zone. S
lieves that if they are exposed to something or someone new, the members of the team might think that
she doesn't really know what she's doing. She needs to
keep her leadership position.

Unfortunately, our ministries are often made up of
people who live in their own version of truth, without
any desire to change or shift to God's ways. Are we
more devoted to our ideas of what truth is and our
ideas of what Jesus wants than we are to Jesus Himself?

> *"The heart is deceitful above all things, and
> desperately wicked: who can know it? I the LORD
> search the heart, I try the reins, even to give
> every man according to his ways, and according
> to the fruit of his doings."* - Jeremiah 17:9-10

Why does God require us to walk in truth? Because
He is a God of truth. And His truth sets us free to worship! Holy Spirit is called the Spirit of Truth. Truth is not
just what God does, it is who He is.

Truth is His. Truth belongs to Him. He only operates
in truth. His actions are truth. Everything He does is
truth. He is a God of truth. God wants us to live, walk,
talk and dance in truth from the deepest part of who
we are.

On Sunday morning at church, you see Sister Smith
coming your way. You really don't like her, but instead

of talking with her and clearing the air, you allow your offense to remain. You greet her with a false smile and ought in your heart. Then you minister in dance. Is that living in truth?

Many times we have bitterness or unforgiveness in our heart towards someone. We see people in church or in the mall and we avoid them, or we lie and say, "So good to see you!" Rather than acknowledge this and ask the Lord to help us, we carry this around and smile in the face of the person we don't like. There is no truth in that, therefore there is no freedom.

A hypocrite is described as an actor under an assumed character, a stage-player—one who decides to pretend, speak or act under a false part. Who are you? Are you covering or hiding the real you? If so, how will you worship?

When the doors close, are you the same as you are on Sundays? In Ezekiel 28, it says that the iniquity was found in the heart of Satan. The word iniquity means dishonesty.

> "But let your communication (what you think, what you say, even what you do) be, Yea, yea; (truth, truth) Nay, nay: for whatsoever is more comes from evil, the devil." - Matthew 5:37

John 8:44 tells us that there is no truth in him. He cannot tell the truth. When he speaks, he speaks of his own nature of who he is—a liar. Therefore, he will never be free.

Lying usually stems from a selfish motive. People lie because of something they want or because of something they feel or something they are hiding to protect.

To lie means to utter an untruth or attempt to deceive by falsehood. So when you lie, you are promoting the kingdom of darkness. There is no truth there. Don't live a lie. Live in truth so you can be free to be uniquely you!

God only operates in truth. All of His works are done in truth. He answers those who call upon Him in truth. That's the realm and the domain that He operates in. And that's why He desires truth in our inward parts.

I read that there are actually four parts to every person:

1. The part that you see and know that other people see and know.
2. The part you see that other people don't see.
3. The part that other people see that you don't see. It's called your blind side.
4. The part that you don't see and other people don't see, only God knows.

It is the work of the Holy Spirit to address those areas of our lives that are inconsistent with the Word of God.

The Spirit of Truth will come to shine the light of God's Word into those dark areas so we can address those areas and be free! Sometimes we rationalize with God. We say, "God, what I meant was..." We must remember—the truth is, He knows exactly what we meant. Never allow anything that divides or destroys God's truth and the oneness of your life with Christ to remain in your life without facing it.

Often we do not want to face the truth because the truth hurts, or the truth will require us to change and most of us don't want to change. Sometimes it's just easier if we just pretend like situations don't exist because the truth hurts too much for us to look at. Then we are not truly free. It might mean that we need to admit to others that we are wrong. If we can't do that, we have to ask ourselves, "Is it pride that keeps us from the truth?"

Truth requires humility, transparency and absolute integrity. There are no gray areas in the truth. Sometimes you can't see the truth until you admit the truth to yourself and to God. Then He can shine His light in that place. That's when true freedom comes. That's spirit and truth.

Psalm 91:4 declares that His truth is our shield and buckler. That means His truth is our protection and it keeps us free. Do you have a heart of stone, unwilling to allow God's truth to change you? Or... do you have a heart of flesh, a heart that is yielded to Holy Spirit? The truth is that you are called to be free and to set others free.

Will you look in the mirror of truth? Mirrors do not lie. Will you let Him expose you to YOU? It's not about anybody else.

Be honest with yourself. Are you dancing to impress others instead of dancing from a place of truth? Are you dancing your issues instead of His messages?

Worship is said to be therapeutic for the worshiper but dance ministry is not meant to be the place where you release your issues for all to see. You must deal with that in your prayer closet.

Our mandate is to minister in spirit and truth. We must hear from heaven, then we can release His message into the earth. That's worship in spirit and truth.

This is the higher call.

Chapter 8

Called to Build
New Altars of Worship

Reading through Genesis, you will see that Abraham built altars to worship the Lord. Why were altars so important? If altars were important to God in the Old Testament, why don't we build and worship at altars today?

Most people consider the altar to be the front of the church. Yet, this is not really the same type of altar at which Abraham worshiped. What is an altar?

Mentioned some 400 times in the Bible, an altar is a place of worship where we offer something to God. It's a place that keeps God as the main focus of one's life. So altars are about worship.

Why build an altar? An altar is the meeting place between the physical and the spiritual. The altar is where the physical contacts the spiritual. When God desires to do a new work, He needs people who are passionate in worship, willing to build new altars.

The altar is also a place of sacrifice. God expects you to build the altar. He expects you to prepare a place where the two of you can meet.

The building of the altar is a matter of your own choice, your own will and it is your responsibility. It's not enough just to be where the altars are being built. You must build your own.

> *"And they that went in, went in male and female of all flesh, as God had commanded him: and the LORD shut him in."* - Genesis 7:16

It was the Lord (Jehovah) who invited Noah and his family into the ark and it was the Lord who shut him in.

After the flood, it was God (Elohim) who gave the command:

> *"And God spake unto Noah, saying, Go forth of the ark, thou, and thy wife, and thy sons, and thy sons' wives with thee."* Genesis 8:15-16

The first mention of an altar is found here:

> *"And Noah builded an altar unto the LORD; and took of every clean beast, and of every clean fowl, and offered burnt offerings on the altar. And the LORD smelled a sweet savour; and the LORD said in his heart, I will not again curse the ground any more for man's sake."*
> - Genesis 8:20-21

As Noah emerges into a new world, his first act is worship. It was a pleasant smell, an acceptable odor, so much that God then said He would not curse the ground any more.

The Hebrew word for altar is mizbeach, a slaughter place. Various materials were used in the construction of an altar, from earth or unhewn stone, to wood covered with bronze.

In the patriarchal period, we find Abraham, Isaac and Jacob building altars at critical points in their lives when God revealed Himself to them. But when the tabernacle was constructed and the temple built, there was only one place where the altar was erected; that was the place where God had placed His name, the gathering center of His people.

True worship takes place in the context of our obedience to God. Abraham was in the process of obeying God's prompting to go to the land of Canaan. We cannot truly worship God unless we are in the place of obedience.

Abraham built altars to worship effectively. Wherever Abraham went—cities, countrysides and villages—he built altars to the Lord God. There he worshiped the Lord. Abraham simply loved God.

If we are going to change history, it will require new altars of worship. Abraham once built an altar at the very site where King David would begin to reign and extend the Kingdom of Israel to its borders. Abraham walked the entire length and breadth of his inheritance. Finally, at Hebron, Abraham sought the Lord and laid claimed to his inheritance for future generations.

Notice what was going on in Abraham's life just before he built this altar of ministry. God allowed him to separate himself from Lot (see Genesis 13:6-14).

"Lots" are merely the people we have in our lives that will potentially ruin any ministry God develops.

Building worship altars requires you to come alone. It is not about anyone else. It is not about being nice and generous to others. Sometimes this even includes family and friends. My husband always says, "There are yesterday people, today people and tomorrow people. The people who were in your yesterday, might not be in your today or your tomorrow. You must know the difference."

We live in the New Testament era of grace, so where are our worship altars? Why is it even important for us to ask? In order to gain forgiveness, acceptance, and access to God, altars were needed. Sacrifices were made on altars. Blood was spilled on altars. This was done that sin might be removed and the worshiper cleansed.

Today, through His blood, we have access anytime to the throne of God. So today, we no longer have need of "altars" in the Old Testament sense. But we do need altars in our lives in another way.

The altar involves surrender and sacrifice. Many people want to worship God in their own way, a way that involves no sacrifice whatsoever. They want to worship as long as it is in their comfort zone.

It is imperative we worship God as He requires, through Jesus Christ, and through Him alone. He is our altar. We are to approach God in and through Him. Not through man-made traditions.

Throughout the Old Testament, altars would be made. Moses' tabernacle had one, as did Solomon's temple. These altars were made of stones. There are altars in the New Testament as well, but in the New Testament, something changes. The altars are made of living stones. The people of God gathered for worship and intercession. When Jesus explained that where two or more are gathered that He was among them, He was changing the way people encountered God altogether.

The access that Jacob dreamed of, a single place on the earth where he met with God, has now been disseminated to the nations. Instead of traveling to the altar, now believers can make an altar or gather and make an altar with two or three in agreement, and God sets down his ladder in the middle of their meeting.

In Genesis 28, Jacob had a dream. You know the story—the ladder, the angels, the King of Glory at the top. When Jacob awakes, the first thing he does is commemorate the significance of finding the "door of heaven" by setting up a stone. He creates an altar.

After all he had been through with Laban, building an altar brought revival in Jacob's life, but first there were certain requirements:

> *"And God said unto Jacob, Arise, go up to Bethel, and dwell there: and make there an altar unto God, that appeared unto thee when thou fleddest from the face of Esau thy brother. Then Jacob said unto his household, and to all that*

were with him, Put away the strange gods that are among you, and be clean, and change your garments: And let us arise, and go up to Bethel; and I will make there an altar unto God, who answered me in the day of my distress, and was with me in the way which I went. And they gave unto Jacob all the strange gods which were in their hand, and all their earrings which were in their ears; and Jacob hid them under the oak which was by Shechem. And they journeyed: and the terror of God was upon the cities that were round about them, and they did not pursue after the sons of Jacob." - Genesis 35:1-5

God said to Jacob:
"Arise."
"Go to Bethel."
"Dwell there."
"Make an altar..."

Jacob told his household and all who were with him, to put away the foreign gods, purify themselves and change their garments. God is saying the same to us. He requires us to put away every idol, purify our hearts and change our garments of flesh for garments of righteousness.

Then they would arise and go up to Bethel and Jacob would make an altar there to God. The Bible goes on to say that "the terror of God was upon the cities that were round about them, and they did not pursue after the sons of Jacob." Building this altar brought God's protection.

God appeared to Jacob again and spoke to him at Bethel. Relationship was restored. He spoke to him about his assignment, his destiny and his identity. An altar is a place to hear from God and receive instruction for the future.

Ultimately, God wanted his heart. And He wants the same from us.

> *"And the children of Israel did evil in the sight of the Lord: and the Lord delivered them into the hand of Midian seven years."* - Judges 6:1

These words describe an endless cycle that repeated itself in Israel for generations. Throughout the preceding chapters, we find these words repeated again and again. They adapted to the demonic structures of their time.

Of course, every time Israel was enslaved, they cried out to God. And each time, the Lord was faithful to send them a deliverer. But as soon as that righteous leader died, the people returned to their sin. And the whole cycle began all over again.

So God sent a prophet who put his finger on the reason the people were being so harassed. Every time God would deliver them, He told them not to fear the gods of the Amorites. But the people didn't obey God. They still paid homage to false gods.

The Lord was telling His people not to fear anyone but Him. Yet, they allowed fear to enter in. He handed them over to their enemies to drive them back to Himself.

In essence, they forsook God and also served Baalim (Judges 10:10). The word Baalim is a plural form. It denotes all the false gods in the world. The root of Baalim is Baal, which is a demonic spirit.

Baal's ultimate mission is to rob God of all worship and trust by His people. It accomplishes this by focusing our attention on our circumstances rather than on the Lord. Baal means master. This spirit seeks to master you.

God is still saying to us today that He desires more from us. The Bible says that Israel wept loudly, crying out to God in their anguish. They acknowledged that they had sinned. But there was yet another step to take to build an altar of worship: tear down Baal.

> *"Take thy father's young bullock, even the second bullock of seven years old, and throw down the altar of Baal that thy father hath, and cut down the grove that is by it."* - Judges 6:25

The Lord spoke that word to Gideon. Gideon probably thought he repented sufficiently. After all, he had cried out to the Lord. He had heard the prophetic word God sent to Israel. And he had responded to it fully, acknowledging his sin.

We see the same thing among many Christians today. We repent, cry out to God and hear the prophetic words. But there is still an idol in our midst: Baal. And before we build new worship altars, we must first tear down any altars of mistrust or unbelief. Otherwise, it won't matter how much we cry out to God, pray or fast. Our actions won't have the impact we need, until we pull down any idols that might be in our heart.

That is a spirit, sent forth from hell for one purpose: to cause people to doubt the reality of God. Ultimately, it is a spirit of mistrust and unbelief. It seeks to assault our minds with doubts about God's faithfulness. Time out for people, places or things that keep us from full surrender in serving God. Left unchallenged, the Baal spirit of unbelief moves in and sets up an altar.

Right now, there is widespread uncertainty in our society. Bankruptcies are at an all-time high. Workers are afraid of losing their jobs. As people look at the future, they're overwhelmed by fear. In times like this, Satan launches an all-out attack. He wants to get into your mind to plant seeds and build a Baal altar. He wants you to doubt everything you've ever known about God's Word.

In Judges 6, an angel brings a word to Gideon, whose name means warrior:

"The Lord is with thee, thou mighty man of valour." - Judges 6:1

The word mighty means gibbor—powerful, warrior, tyrant, champion, mighty one, strong man, valiant man. Valour is the word Chayil, meaning a force, an army, wealth, virtue, strength, ability, activity, power, riches, strength, strong, substance, valiant, war worthy. Chayil comes the word chuwl, meaning to dance. It can be read this way:

"You mighty, powerful, warrior, tyrant:- You champion, You excel, You are a giant, mighty, valiant man. I have made you to be a force, an army, with wealth, virtue, valor, strength:--you are able. You have my might, my power, my riches, my strength, my substance. I have made you war, worthy. So dance!"

God speaks the same words to us: "The Lord is with you." The Lord is saying, "My promise is all you need: I am with you. Dance!"

God had already commanded Gideon, "Go, deliver Israel. I will be with you." But there was still a heart issue to deal with.

The Lord told Gideon, "You still have doubts that I'm with you. Now go, get your father's bull, and pull down that idol. Then cut down all the trees in the grove, and use them to build a new altar. You're going to consume your father's idol on that altar. I want you to bring down that symbol of unbelief and destroy it completely." When Gideon pulled down the altar of Baal in his father house, the worshipers of Baal rose up against him but the Almighty God delivered him from them all.

God is about to do a new, powerful work in our lives. He is bringing us into new victories. He's about to do a new thing. But first, you must pull down every thought of doubt, and lay down every fear. God wants you to tear down the spirit of Baal completely in your heart, and begin to live and speak in faith.

Put the enemy on notice. Say, "God is with me, devil. You can't hurt me. And you can't stop His plans for my life. The Lord has victories ahead for me."

God required the same of Elijah. When Ahab and Jezebel were passionate about instituting their false religion, they erected an altar to Baal. This shows us the devil's intentions. He wanted to establish his own altar at the place that should have been dedicated to God.

Elijah gathered all of Israel together. God told him rain was coming on the earth but the rain couldn't come until the altar was repaired. His job was to repair the altar that had been broken down. He then challenged the people of Israel.

"And Elijah came unto all the people, and said, How long halt ye between two opinions? if the LORD be God, follow him: but if Baal, then follow

him. And the people answered him not a word."
- 1 Kings 18:21

The word halt means to do a limping dance. He was essentially asking, "How long will you dance between two opinions?"

It says they answered him not a word. He set up the altar and challenged the prophets of Baal to call on their god. The Bible says they leaped and danced before their altar all day long but no one heard them.

God said, "Build an altar to Me. Call on Me! I will answer by fire and everyone will know that I am the Lord. I am God."

"And call ye on the name of your gods, and I will call on the name of the LORD: and the God that answereth by fire, let him be God. And all the people answered and said, It is well spoken."
- 1 Kings 18:24

There had been no rain for three and a half years. I'm sure these false prophets had cried out to their gods for intervention, but just as Baal couldn't send the fire from heaven, he was unable to send the rain either.

When you build a new altar to God, it is then when you begin to hear the sound of abundance. Just as God was faithful to send the rain for Elijah, He will send it for you and me as well. If we follow Elijah's example, the heavens will open and the rain will fall.

Build a new altar of worship. The fire of God will fall and consume anything in our lives that is not like Him. Because after the fire, we are promised the rain. If we desire the rain of heaven in our lives, then it is time to rebuild the altar of the Lord!

Build an altar of worship. Receive answers to your prayers. When you have repaired the altar of God and built a new one, then your offering shall be accepted of the Lord.

When the fire fell on Mt. Carmel, it was not only the firewood that was consumed, it also consumed the stones. The symbol of hardship was removed. The fire licked up the water. Not only that, the fire also consumed the dust that was on the ground. The dust represents the flesh. When you do what God asked you to do, when you build this new altar to God, the grace to overcome the things that caused us to war in the works of the flesh will be released.

When this fire fell, everybody fell on their faces and acknowledged God.

> *"And when all the people saw it, they fell on their faces: and they said, The LORD, he is the God; the LORD, he is the God."* - 1 Kings 18:39

In a single a moment, a whole nation turned to God. The altar was the priority.

Even the altar of sacrifice where you met with God today will be old tomorrow, so build a new one. Don't settle for the altars of yesterday. Build new ones.

It's not enough for us to tear down pagan altars and remove the priests of Baal. We must repair the Lord's altar and cry out for new fire from heaven that consumes the burnt offerings. We must be jealous for the honor of God's house and not hesitate to obey Him.

The new altar that we must build to God must be:

1. An altar of faith. Stop doubting God.

> *"But without faith it is impossible to please him: for he that cometh to God must believe that he is, and that he is a rewarder of them that diligently seek him."* - Hebrews 11:6

Is there anything too hard for God? No! What God has spoken, He will bring to pass. Build an altar of faith. Every promise of God concerning you shall be fulfilled.

2. An altar of thanksgiving and praise. It's still an altar of sacrifice.

> *"By him therefore let us offer the sacrifice of praise to God continually, that is, the fruit of our lips giving thanks to his name. And do not forget*

to do good and to share with others, for with such sacrifices God is pleased."

- Hebrews 13:15-16

Let it be an altar of thanksgiving, learn to thank Him; thank Him for what He has done and thank Him because He is about to do a new thing!

"Remember ye not the former things, neither consider the things of old. Behold, I will do a new thing; now it shall spring forth; shall ye not know it? I will even make a way in the wilderness, and rivers in the desert. This people have I formed for myself; they shall shew forth my praise." - Isaiah 43:18-21

3. An altar of worship.

"Praise waiteth for thee, O God, in Sion: and unto thee shall the vow be performed. O thou that hearest prayer, unto thee shall all flesh come. Iniquities prevail against me: as for our transgressions, thou shalt purge them away. Blessed is the man whom thou choosest, and causest to approach unto thee, that he may dwell in thy courts: we shall be satisfied with the goodness of thy house, even of thy holy temple."

- Psalm 65:1-4

"Come, let us bow down in worship, let us kneel before the LORD our Maker; for he is our God and we are the people of his pasture, the flock under his care." - Psalm 95:6-4

4. An altar that exalts God.

"Let God arise, let his enemies be scattered: let them also that hate him flee before him. As smoke is driven away, so drive them away: as wax melteth before the fire, so let the wicked perish at the presence of God." - Psalm 68:1-2

Build your altar. The presence of the Lord will come to destroy the works of the enemy.

5. An altar to call upon the Lord.

"I will call upon the LORD, who is worthy to be praised: so shall I be saved from mine enemies."
- Psalm 18:3

When you worship Him and you begin to call upon His name, He will rise on your behalf and save you from your enemies.

6. An altar of prayer.

"Call unto me, and I will answer thee, and shew thee great and mighty things, which thou knowest not." - Jeremiah 33:3

The altar of God must be an altar of prayer. He promises to answer prayer. He said He will answer you, not He might, but He will.

7. An altar of sacrifice!

You must build an altar of sacrifice. When you learn to sacrifice to God, get ready for envy. When God responds to your sacrifice, those who don't know your sacrifice will become envious of you.

Until you yourself become a living sacrifice, then the altar is not yet built. Make yourself a living sacrifice! If you are too big to be a sacrifice on the altar of God, then you are definitely too big!

Build new altars. The mighty God will answer you by fire. He will accept you as a living sacrifice to Himself. God will build a wall of fire round about you. He will send help to you, even help from heaven above.

Build new altars and those who are pursuing you will never be able to overtake you. Worship from the deepest place of who you are. Worship like you know that all you have came from God.

Don't give Him just a convenient worship. Get lost in the presence of God. Receive all from the presence of

God until His presence makes you forget all else except the God who gave it all to you.

This is our higher call!

Chapter 9
Called to Be a Gatekeeper

The Bible speaks much about gates. Just as there are gatekeepers in the natural realm, God has called us to be gatekeepers in the spiritual realm. When you fly on an airplane, you cannot board the plane unless you have a ticket. The ticket agents act as gatekeepers. Their job is to keep anyone off the plane who may cause any harm.

During biblical times, the gatekeepers were very important. In 1 Chronicles 9, the gatekeepers were mentioned with the singers and musicians. They were appointed and chosen by the king and they had daily responsibilities in the temple. They had to be loyal and trustworthy. They were responsible for the safety of the temple.

There were keepers of the temple gates and keepers of the city gates. They were able to refuse or admit entrance to anyone. They were in place for the protection of the temple or the city.

> "And Shallum the son of Kore, the son of Ebiasaph, the son of Korah, and his brethren, of the house of his father, the Korahites, were over the work of the service, keepers of the gates of the tabernacle: and their fathers, being over the host of the LORD, were keepers of the entry. And

Phinehas the son of Eleazar was the ruler over them in time past, and the LORD was with him. And Zechariah the son of Meshelemiah was porter of the door of the tabernacle of the congregation. All these which were chosen to be porters in the gates were two hundred and twelve. These were reckoned by their genealogy in their villages, whom David and Samuel the seer did ordain in their set office. So they and their children had the oversight of the gates of the house of the LORD, namely, the house of the tabernacle, by wards. In four quarters were the porters, toward the east, west, north, and south. And their brethren, which were in their villages, were to come after seven days from time to time with them. For these Levites, the four chief porters, were in their set office, and were over the chambers and treasuries of the house of God. And they lodged round about the house of God, because the charge was upon them, and t he opening thereof every morning pertained to them." - 1 Chronicles 9:19-27

The Bible mentions several references to gates:

"Enter ye in at the strait gate: for wide is the gate, and broad is the way, that leadeth to destruction, and many there be which go in thereat: Because strait is the gate, and narrow is

the way, which leadeth unto life, and few there be that find it." - Matthew 7:13-14

"And I say also unto thee, That thou art Peter, and upon this rock I will build my church; and the gates of hell shall not prevail against it."
- Matthew 16:18

"Enter into his gates with thanksgiving, and into his courts with praise: be thankful unto him, and bless his name." - Psalm 100:4

We learn from these verses that heaven has gates and hell has gates. In the natural, gates and walls were built for the protection of the city. When one was said to possess the gate of his enemy, it meant that the person had gained a position of wealth and power over the enemy. When the gates and the walls were torn down or broken down, it gave access for the enemy to come in.

There were city gates and there were temple gates. Even as the Bible speaks of literal gates, the first gates we need to be keepers of are the gates of our very lives.

"What? know ye not that your body is the temple of the Holy Ghost which is in you, which ye have of God, and ye are not your own?"
- 1 Corinthians 6:19

We must protect what comes into His temple through our ear gates, our eye gates, our mouth gate, our nose gate and even the gate of our skin. We must be careful what we touch. We must also protect the gateway to our physical intimacy.

What are we watching on television? What kind of music are we listening to? What are we eating? We must protect the temple of God and then become those who protect our families and homes. This speaks of being gatekeepers in the realm of the spirit.

> *"Blessed is the man that heareth me, watching daily at my gates, waiting at the posts of my doors. For whoso findeth me findeth life, and shall obtain favour of the LORD."*
>
> *- Proverbs 8:34-35*

Are you watching daily at His gates? A biblical gatekeeper is one who guards access to a place:

A residence:

> *"Then saith the damsel that kept the door unto Peter, Art not thou also one of this man's disciples? He saith, I am not."* - John 18:17

The Ark:

> *"So they brought the ark of God, and set it in the midst of the tent that David had pitched for it:*

and they offered burnt sacrifices and peace offerings before God." - 1 Chronicles 16:1

The temple:

"And to stand every morning to thank and praise the LORD, and likewise at even; And that they should keep the charge of the tabernacle of the congregation, and the charge of the holy place, and the charge of the sons of Aaron their brethren, in the service of the house of the LORD." - 1 Chronicles 23:30, 32

The city:

"And David sat between the two gates: and the watchman went up to the roof over the gate unto the wall, and lifted up his eyes, and looked, and behold a man running alone."

- 2 Samuel 18:24

The city gates were places of assembly. At the city gates they conducted business and the elders gathered there to make important decisions concerning the city and people.

The city gates were where the people assembled for social and legal matters to be settled. It was a place for marketing, business, reading and teaching the law. It was a place to attract the notice of the king and gain an audience with him. It was a place of authority and punishment and the place where the prophetic word came forth.

I believe God has called us all to be keepers of spiritual gates. We must place ourselves at the gates of our home, our church, our city and our nation. Let us take our positions at the gates through prayer, intercession, dancing, praise, worship and speaking the Word of God. This is our higher call.

Nehemiah is a book about restoration. It tells us the story of a man who had been placed by God as the cupbearer to the king, yet he gave up a high position to identify with the plight of his people.

At the time of Nehemiah, Jerusalem was the spiritual and political center of Judah. In chapter one, we read that his countrymen came to him to report that Nebuchadnezzar had destroyed the walls of Jerusalem and the gates had been burned with fire.

> "I asked them concerning the Jews who had escaped, who had survived the captivity, and concerning Jerusalem. And they said to me, 'The survivors who are left from the captivity in the province are there in great distress and reproach. The wall of Jerusalem is also broken down, and its GATES are burned with fire."
>
> - Nehemiah 1:2-3

valls, it could hardly be considered a city. It was open to enemy attack and ungodly influences.

Upon hearing this news, the Bible says that Nehemiah wept, fasted and prayed to the God of Heaven. After receiving permission to go to inspect the gates, he then called the people together to repair the gates that had been destroyed.

Nehemiah went to Jerusalem and saw that the gates of protection and authority in his city were burned with fire. May I suggest that many gates of the present-day church have been burned with fire yet many of us do not open our eyes to see the need or are not willing to do the work necessary for rebuilding.

In many churches, it is business as usual... Sunday after Sunday. Our laziness, lethargy, selfishness, traditions, backbiting, jealousy, competitive spirit and sins have allowed our gates to be destroyed and left us vulnerable to enemy attacks. We need to listen for God's voice—look and see in the spirit realm and be repairers of the gates in our own lives, our families, our churches and our nation.

What gates are in need of repair? First, let us repair the gates of a holy walk with God so we can go forth to do His works in the earth (Psalm 118:19-20). Let us repair the gates of salvation for the harvest to come in. Let us repair the gates of revelation and prophetic anointing with repentance, humility and cleansing with God's Word.

In the Old Testament, we see that the ⊦
washed, made sacrifices and were sanctified at the
ple gates. I believe this also speaks of the local church.
2 Chronicles 31:2 says the priests were appointed to
stand and give thanks and praise.

As New Testament priests, we must learn to stand
and give thanks and praise and offer spiritual sacrifices
to our God. Let us come to the house of God with no
agenda, other than to seek Him. Let us cry out for Him
and give way to Him. Let us yearn for that which is real,
not that which is manufactured. Man cannot duplicate
what God gives by His Spirit. Let us yearn to see God
and to hear Him.

Because praise and worship is an entrance into the
presence of God, it is a gate that is often in need of
repair. Praise and worship establishes the Kingdom of
God in the earth. Let us empty our songs and make way
for His songs. Let us empty our dances and make way
for His dances.

God has a purpose for every time we gather together. Our culture breeds performance. We often see
talent and call it the anointing. Let us become aware of
the goings of God in the midst of His people.

It is not the job of praise and worship leaders to sing
the latest songs. It is their job to lift the heavy burdens
off of the people as they come into the Lord's house so
they can be free to offer praise to God. It is their job to
minister and sing over the people—to be lifters of
burdens.

As my friend Vivien Hibbert says, "Psalmist are carriers of the words of God, musicians are carriers of the sounds of God and dancers are carriers of the sights of God." Let us be those words, sounds and sights at the gates, that God may visit us in Spirit and in Truth, that we might see the gates of the church repaired.

In 2 Chronicles 23:19, the gatekeepers were in place so nothing unclean could enter in. We need to be the authority at the gates. Let us pray, speak God's Word, sing and dance over the lives of our families and leaders. Let us take God's Word in our mouths and prophesy God's Word, sing God's Word, and dance God's Word.

We can go to the literal gates of a city, but we can also go in the spirit realm. Let us be responsible to minister at the gates through praise, worship, prayer and intercession. Where there are people of righteousness, praise and the prophetic word of God, the spiritual climate of a family, city or nation can be affected for God's purposes. The rebuilding of the walls (our prayer life) and the gates (our natural and spiritual openings) are found in Nehemiah Chapter 3.

As stated earlier, there were city gates and there were temple gates. The temple gates can be representative of our natural body as well as the body of Christ in a corporate context.

I believe that if the church of Jesus Christ will take their positions at the gates, we can see restoration even as Nehemiah did. Nehemiah stayed focused and true to the vision and the assignment of rebuilding the walls and repairing the gates. He called the people together in a spirit of unity. In spite of opposition, Nehemiah and the people accomplished the task in record time. As a result, all the people were blessed and worshiped the Lord.

God brought a great deliverance. The covenant was renewed, the wall was dedicated and the people separated themselves from sin. Complete restoration was the end result. Old destructive cycles were reversed and new cycles of blessings were experienced by all.

We see another example of this in the life of Esther. At the time of Esther, we read that the enemy had plotted and planned evil against God's people. We read that Mordecai was gathered at the gate and it was at the gate that he overheard this evil plot. He then told Esther, who in turn fasted and prayed for three days. She had access to the king, but first and most importantly, she had access to THE KING who had given her a strategy for victory.

In these last days, God is positioning us at the gate in prayer so that He can expose the plans of the enemy and give us a strategy to overcome every time. As we place ourselves at the gates, God will show us how to overthrow the plans of the enemy that would try to stop us from advancing personally and corporately.

To close the gates of hell, we must first open the gates of Heaven. Light overcomes darkness. Let's enter

His gates with thanksgiving and His courts with praise. Praise opens the gates of heaven.

Let's use the authority God has given us, take our positions at the gates and become visual demonstrations of what God is saying and doing to release His plans into the earth. Our feet represent authority and He has said He would give us every piece of ground our feet tread upon. He has given us the necks of our enemies and makes the enemy like ashes under the soles of our feet.

Our hands also represent authority. We raise them to God in surrender and we clap them unto Him in praise. But we also clap them together to smite the enemy. The enemy knows the difference in a clap of praise and one that is intended as a weapon of our warfare.

We shout unto God with a voice of triumph! We shout BECAUSE the enemy is defeated, not to defeat him. Jesus has already accomplished that on our behalf. Colossians 2:15 says "Jesus has spoiled principalities and powers and made a show of them openly!" Victory is ours if we will only take our positions at the gates.

This is our higher call!

SECTION

2

Chapter 10
The Sights, Signs and Sounds Mandate

CALLED TO BE THE SIGHTS, THE SIGNS AND THE SOUNDS

The remaining chapters will discuss our mandate to be the sights, the signs and the sounds of God in the earth, revealing Him to a lost and dying world.

Vivien Hibbert is an amazing worship leader. She teaches that dancers are "carriers of the sights of God." I took that to mean that we are responsible for hearing from heaven and then, through our movements, we reveal what God is saying to us in the earth realm.

People should be able to see our movements and understand what God is saying. We must go from movement only to the revelation of what God is saying. Then we reveal the revelation through the movement. That's how we become the sights of God. That's our mandate as ministers of the Gospel. A mandate is an official order or commission to do something.

Consider the meaning of the word mandate:

- A directive, a decree, a command, an order, an injunction, an edict, a charge or a ruling.

- A commission by which a party is entrusted to perform a service, especially without payment and with indemnity against loss by that party.

- An order from an appellate court to a lower court to take a specific action.

- A written authority enabling someone to carry out transactions on another's bank account.

- The authority to carry out a policy or course of action, regarded as given by the electorate to a candidate or party that is victorious in an election.

- The authority given to someone to act in a certain way.

> *"And on the seventh day God ended his work which he had made; and he rested on the seventh day from all his work which he had made. And God blessed the seventh day, and sanctified it: because that in it he had rested from all his work which God created and made. And the LORD God formed man of the dust of the ground, and breathed into his nostrils the breath of life; and man became a living soul. And the LORD God planted a garden eastward in Eden; and there he put the man whom he had*

formed. And out of the ground made the LORD God to grow every tree that is pleasant to the sight, and good for food; the tree of life also in the midst of the garden, and the tree of knowledge of good and evil." - Genesis 2:2-9

The word Eden translates as pleasure or delight. Eden means the house of pleasure. In this place of pleasure and delight, God brought forth every tree— trees pleasant to the sight and good for food.

The word sight means a shape, especially if it's a handsome or beautiful shape. It's speaking here of appearance. It also means, to see, to have vision, countenance, fair, favoured, good to look upon.

The trees were said to be pleasant to look at in the sight of others, literally, lovely to see; i.e. beautiful in form and color. The trees were good for food. In other words, not only did it look pleasant but it was able to provide sustenance to minister to corporeal necessities.

Hence, the pleasant place of the Lord was the highest ideal of earthly excellence. In particular, it was distinguished by the presence of two trees, which occupied a central position. The tree of life, and the tree of knowledge of good and evil.

The tree of life was so called from its symbolic character as a sign of immortal life. It might be also a sign, token, and symbol to man of his dependence on God; that man received his life from Him; and life is preserved by His blessing and providence, and not by his own power and skill.

The tree of the knowledge of good and evil was so called because it was a test of obedience. The tree was a testing place. It tried them—whether they would obey God or break His commands.

Which tree are you? What does it have to do with us and our mandate to be the sights of God? These trees can be seen as an emblem of the saints—the trees of righteousness, the planting of the Lord, who are made to grow by Him through the influence of His Spirit and grace.

The Bible compares saints to palm trees, cedar trees, olive trees and more. For now, let's look quickly at olive trees.

OLIVE TREES

"But as for me, I am like a green olive tree in the house of God; I trust in the lovingkindness of God forever and ever." - Psalm 52:8

The olive tree primarily symbolizes faithfulness and steadfastness. No matter what the conditions: hot, dry, cold, wet, rocky, or sandy, the evergreen olive tree will live and produce fruit.

What test are you going through? Are you in a hot season, a dry season, a wet season, a rocky season or a season full of sand? Whatever season you are in, do you feel that you have to let the whole world know about it? Some choose to talk to people instead of God. They rehearse the situation to anyone who will listen.

> *"The fool vents all his feelings, but the wise person keeps them to himself."*
> - Proverbs 29:11 (ISV)

It is said that you can never kill an olive tree. Even when cut down or burned, new shoots will emerge from its roots. How do you react under various conditions? You can either let the trial kill you or you can arise with new life.

No matter what the conditions of life, we should remain steadfast as the olive tree in the presence of God—always green, faithful and bearing fruit. They not only provide oxygen for us to breathe, but also food to eat, wood for building houses and furniture, pulp for paper, fuel for warmth, and shade for rest and recreation.

In their great variety, trees provide natural beauty for our eyes to behold. How do you look? Man looks at the outward appearance but God looks at the heart. However, that doesn't mean you can present yourself any kind of way.

Queen of Sheba came to Solomon... first it says when she heard about him, she decided she had to go see for herself and she brought camels filled with riches.

> "When the queen of Sheba had seen all Solomon's wisdom and skill, the house he had built, The food of his table, the seating of his officials, the standing at attention of his servants, their apparel, his cupbearers, his ascent by which he went up to the house of the Lord [or the burnt offerings he sacrificed], she was breathless and overcome. She said to the king, It was a true report I heard in my own land of your acts and sayings and wisdom. I did not believe it until I came and my eyes had seen. Behold, the half was not told me. You have added wisdom and goodness exceeding the fame I heard."
>
> - 1 Kings 10:4-7

What will people hear about your ministry and what will they see once they arrive? Will they see a spirit of excellence, clothed with beauty, grace, strength and honor?

> "Consider how the wild flowers grow. They do not labor or spin. Yet I tell you, not even Solomon in all his splendor was dressed like one of these." - Luke 12:27

God is so detailed, even the wildflowers are beautiful!

When you minister, are your garments clean? Are they pressed or do they have wrinkles? How did you care for them? Do they fit properly? Are they too tight? Did you comb your hair or does it have its own choreography?

> *"The righteous shall flourish like the palm tree: he shall grow like a cedar in Lebanon."*
>
> - Psalm 92:12

PALM TREES

1) Grow Upright

A palm tree grows straight up. It has no branches. Always looking up towards heaven, the palm tree grows to great heights, sometimes even a hundred feet! Rooted in a land, whether fertile or not, it grows up, sucking the moisture from the earth.

2) Each and Every Part is Useful

The palm tree is known for its usefulness. From top to bottom, each and every part of the tree is useful. What purpose are you serving?

3) A Tree Not Affected by Drought

Whatever the weather conditions may be, the palm tree is not affected in any way unless you cut it down. But the life of the palm tree, however, is not affected by any surface injury.

4) Evergreen Tree

The palm tree is green throughout all seasons. Life continually flows within it and keeps it fresh. Rain may fall. Storms may shake and sway the tree with great force. But nothing happens to the palm tree.

5) Inability to Graft

Here's an interesting fact about the palm tree: it is impossible to graft a palm tree into another palm tree. It has its own identity. If you try to graft it in, it will die. Don't compare yourself with anyone. When people see you, do they see you or a copy of someone you think you should be?

6) An Emblem of Victory

Palm branches were carried as tokens of victory. This we see in the triumphant march of Jesus into the city of Jerusalem. Do people see victory when they see you? Can you be sent out and seen as a token of victory?

7) Palm Trees Have Deep Roots

The palm tree has a very acute sense of finding a water resource. Its roots go deep to find water, even in dry places. Even in a desert filled with hot sand, the palm tree survives bearing the scorching heat of the sun.

8) The Palm Tree is Softest at the Heart.

It flourishes in deserts, withstands storms and its fruit gets sweeter with age.

CEDAR TREES

Cedar trees are not only attractive trees, but they also provide an aromatic fragrance. In other words, they look good and smell good. They are tall, they live long and they serve a variety of uses.

Are you only useful when it's time for you to dance? Are you useful to lead prayer? Are you useful to help other people with whatever they might need? He plants us as trees to be sights in His gardens: in the church, in our family, on our job, in our city, state or nation and in the nations.

Whoever you are, wherever you are and whatever you are doing, you are still a sight.

> *"The fruit of the righteous is a tree of life, and the one who is wise saves lives."*
> - Proverbs 11:30 (NIV)

> *"The soothing tongue is a tree of life, but a perverse tongue crushes the spirit."*
> - Proverbs 15:4 (NIV)

Which tree are you? What do people see when they see you? Not only are the trees to be good to look at but we must produce fruit that's good for food.

> *"Behold, I and the children whom the LORD hath given me are for signs and for wonders in Israel from the LORD of hosts, which dwelleth in mount Zion."* - Isaiah 8:18

We are for signs and wonders in the sense of appearing, being seen—a signal, a flag, a beacon, in the sense of conspicuousness. Your life should be seen as conspicuous evidence of the life of God at all times.

PRAISE

> *"The Spirit of the Lord GOD is upon me; because the LORD hath anointed me to preach good tidings unto the meek; he hath sent me to bind up the brokenhearted, to proclaim liberty to the captives, and the opening of the prison to them that are bound; To proclaim the acceptable year of the LORD, and the day of vengeance of our God; to comfort all that mourn; To appoint unto them that mourn in Zion, to give unto them beauty for ashes, the oil of joy for mourning, the garment of praise for the spirit of heaviness; that they might be called (strong) trees of righteous-*

ness, the planted (in the garden) of the LORD,
that he might be glorified." - Isaiah 61:1-3

Be the sight that is a garment of praise for someone's spirit of heaviness. To be a sight of God is more
than good choreography. It's more than knowing when
to do the right dance movement. It's more than looking
glorious in your garments. Being a sight of God has to
do with the heart because we will all see what fruit is on
your tree.

HEALING

Both Ezekiel and Revelation say the same thing about
the trees:

> *"Lining each side of the river banks, all sorts of*
> *species of fruit trees will be growing. Their leaves*
> *will never wither and their fruit will never fail.*
> *They will bear fruit every month, because the*
> *water that nourishes them will be flowing from*
> *the sanctuary. Their fruit will be for food and*
> *their leaves will contain substances that promote*
> *healing."* - Ezekiel 47:12

> *"And he shewed me a pure river of water of life,*
> *clear as crystal, proceeding out of the throne of*
> *God and of the Lamb. In the midst of the street*
> *of it, and on either side of the river, was there*

the tree of life, which bare twelve manner of fruits, and yielded her fruit every month: and the leaves of the tree were for the healing of the nations." - Revelation 22:1-2

When we see you coming, we should say, "Here comes healing!" This is our mandate.

FREEDOM

"Is not this the fast that I have chosen? To loose the bands of wickedness, to undo the heavy burdens, and to let the oppressed go free, and that ye break every yoke?" - Isaiah 58:6

Loose is the Hebrew word nathar: to jump, i.e. be violently agitated; to terrify, shake off, untie:--drive asunder, leap, let loose, make, move, undo. When you jump and turn, you should be the sight of nathar, setting the captives free. This is our mandate.

LIFE

"And the blood shall be to you for a token upon the houses where ye are: and when I see the blood, I will (hop, skip,leap) pass over you, and the plague shall not be upon you to destroy you, when I smite the land of Egypt." - Exodus 12:13

When you leap, you should be the sight of life because the death angel has passed over you. This is our mandate.

DELIVERANCE

> *"For by thee I have run through a troop; and by my God have I leaped over a wall."* - Psalm 18:29

When you run, freedom and deliverance should come because by God you are able to run through troops and leap over walls. This is our mandate.

VICTORY

> *"And having spoiled principalities and powers, he made a shew of them openly, triumphing over them in it."* - Colossians 2:15

Meaning, he took the keys and marched to victory. If someone you know is going through hell, march in and take the keys! Lead them to victory. You are healing to the nations! When you march, be the sight of victory. This is our mandate.

JOY

> *"Praise ye the LORD. Praise God in his sanctuary: praise him in the firmament of his power. Praise*

him for his mighty acts: praise him according to his excellent greatness. Praise him with the sound of the trumpet: praise him with the psaltery and harp. Praise him with the timbrel and dance: praise him with stringed instruments and organs. Praise him upon the loud cymbals: praise him upon the high sounding cymbals. Let every thing that hath breath praise the LORD. Praise ye the LORD." - Psalm 150:1-6

Praise is the Hebrew word halal, meaning to be clear (orig. of sound, but usually of color); to shine; hence, to make a show, to boast; and thus to be (clamorously) foolish; to rave; causatively, to celebrate; also to stultify:--boast (self), celebrate, commend, glory, give (light), be (make, feign self) mad (against), sing, be worthy of praise, rage, renowned, shine. Be the sight, sound and color of joyful praise. This is our mandate.

DANCE OVER THE WILDERNESS

"The voice of The Lord shakes the wilderness."
- Psalm 29:8

The word "shakes" is translated as chuwl, meaning to twist or whirl in a circular or spiral manner, specifically, to dance. That tells me that the voice of the Lord dances over our wilderness. Be the sight of power that dances others out of their wilderness places.

THE SIGHTS, SIGNS AND SOUNDS MANDATE

TRUST

The same word, chuwl, can even mean to trust. You should be the sight of God to encourage someone to trust in God because His judgment will come against their enemies.

REJOICING and HOPE

Be the sight of rejoicing when someone feels like the enemy is closing in on them! When God buried all of their enemies in the Red Sea, they rejoiced! Be the sight of hope.

> "Let us be glad and rejoice, and give honour to him: for the marriage of the Lamb is come, and his wife hath made herself ready."
>
> > - Revelation 19:7

Rejoice means to jump for joy. Be the sight of rejoicing! This is our mandate.

HOPE

> "Now also we would not have you ignorant, brethren, about those who fall asleep in death, that you may not grieve [for them] as the rest do who have no hope beyond the grave."
>
> > - 1 Thessalonians 4:14

Be sight of healing and hope when people are grieving. Hear from heaven, then become the demonstration. Become the sight it in the earth. This is our mandate.

BREAKTHROUGH

> *"But when the Philistines heard that they had anointed David king over Israel, all the Philistines came up to seek David; and David heard of it, and went down to the hold. The Philistines also came and spread themselves in the valley of Rephaim. And David enquired of the LORD, saying, Shall I go up to the Philistines? wilt thou deliver them into mine hand? And the LORD said unto David, Go up: for I will doubtless deliver the Philistines into thine hand. And David came to Baalperazim, and David smote them there, and said, The LORD hath broken forth upon mine enemies before me, as the breach of waters. Therefore he called the name of that place Baalperazim."* - 2 Samuel 5:17-20

"Philistine" means to roll, to wallow in self. The word "Rephaim" translates as invigorating giant.

David asked, "Shall I go up?" To "go up" is the Hebrew word alah, meaning to ascend in worship. God told David to go up! Ascend in worship! He would doubtless deliver them into his hands.

"And the Philistines came up yet again, and spread themselves in the valley of Rephaim. And when David enquired of the LORD, he said, Thou shalt not go up; but fetch a compass behind them, and come upon them over against the mulberry trees. And let it be, when thou hearest the sound of a going in the tops of the mulberry trees, that then thou shalt bestir thyself: for then shall the LORD go out before thee, to smite the host of the Philistines." - 2 Samuel 5:22-24

God gave them a different strategy. He told them to go behind them. Your movement will come when and where it's least expected by the enemy. We can't keep dancing the same way.

God said, "What was can no longer be. Allow Me to move in a new way. Allow Me to make all things new." We can no longer have movement for the sake of movement without the life of God.

David could have expected God to bring victory the same way He did the first time but He enquired of the Lord both times and got a different answer from God both times. We cannot keep doing yesterday's dances—being yesterday's sights when God has a new plan; a new strategy.

This time, God said don't move until you hear the sound of the going in the tops of the trees. Another translation says until you hear the sound of marching, the sound of stepping—meaning when the motion of

113

the agitated leaves simulated the sound of steps, the stepping of men, then David and his army were to step forth to battle.

When the sound from the trees was one with the marching of the army, God came and divinely intervened. The sound was in the trees. The sound brought the movement forth. You have to know when to move out and when to wait for the sound. There are times when the movement has to wait for the sound. Then you become the sight. Then stir yourself.

David waited until God moved; he moved then, but not until then. He was trained to be dependent on God. God honored David and gave him the victory. He had supernatural directions. You can't lean to your own understanding or depend on how God moved before, even if you are ministering the same song as you have in the past.

In the spirit realm, we must listen, observe and obey the motions of the Spirit. Then we advance quickly. It was interesting that these were Mulberry trees. They get their name from fruit that grows on them. These trees require a lot of sunlight. They are resilient to such challenges as drought, pollution and difficult soil. Mulberry trees are not prone to problems with pests and diseases.

And so, David defeated the Philistines both times. When someone needs a breakthrough, you become the sight. This is our mandate.

The Word of God is filled with His sights. In Exodus 15:20, the dances of Miriam and the children of Israel were the sights of God's victory over the enemy. In the New Testament, the father received his prodigal son home with sights and sounds.

> *"Now his elder son was in the field: and as he came and drew nigh to the house, he heard musick and dancing."* - Luke 15:25

The sights and sounds of dancing are the sights of God's love.

This is the mandate of our higher call.

CHAPTER 11

Called to the Glory Realm

The revelation of God begins with the face of Jesus Christ and continues with the glories of heaven. And there is a glory realm that we can enter into that will allow us to see the earth from heaven's perspective. If we live so long on this earthly level, we will see things totally out of perspective and it will affect the way we worship.

I read that when Jim Irwin went to the moon, the thing that amazed him was that the earth appeared to be the size of a golf ball. He said it was life-changing for him. He determined that if God could love the small earth so much he was willing to send His Son, then he would return to earth from his trip to the moon and dedicate his life to the ministry. He also carried a golf ball with him wherever he went as a reminder of that perspective.

The enemy is also a magnifier. He magnifies things out of proportion. Often times, our prayer life and even our worship can be guided by incorrect magnification and not by heaven's viewpoint. So when we are lifted into the glory realm and we see the Lord we always end up with a new perspective.

Let's get heaven's perspective... Heaven's perspective is the perspective of glory. Glory can only be seen through a surrendered life. The glory changes everything. The glory changes our perspective. The glory changes our priorities. We will see as He sees. And we will understand the purpose of prayer and the purpose of worship if we see it from the perspective of the glory realm. When the glory comes, it disrupts what we consider to be normal.

In the realm of glory, our faith is released to believe for greater things. In the realm of glory, we will know the King of Glory and we will know that not only is He the one who fights our battles and brings us victory, but He is the One who rejoices over us as we worship Him. The glory brings proper perspective.

What is the glory realm? It's the realm of eternity. It's the revelation of the presence of God. It's the manifestation of His presence. He is glory. He is everywhere, but His glory is the manifestation of that reality.

Earth has the atmosphere of air but the heavenly atmosphere is glory because His presence is there. When glory comes down to earth's atmosphere, it's a bit of heaven's atmosphere coming down to us. Then we can experience the fragrance of His manifested presence.

> *"And the LORD will create upon every dwelling place of mount Zion, and upon her assemblies, a cloud and smoke by day, and the shining of a flaming fire by night: for upon all the glory shall be a defence or a covering."* - Isaiah 4:5

In the midst of the chaos around us, we are beginning to see the glorious day of the Lord. Every day we can experience this glory. Since glory is the inheritance of every believer, let's not live beneath the place God has for us.

> *"But we all, with open face beholding as in a glass the glory of the Lord, are changed into the same image from glory to glory, even as by the Spirit of the Lord."* - 2 Corinthians 3:18

The glory realm will make you lay aside a lot of petty things that you might've thought to be important. It will make you see things that are really meaningless in the light of eternity.

I believe that in this glory realm, we will be more conscious of his Holiness. God is altogether "Other" than we are. I believe that's why Revelation 4:8 tells us that the four beasts cry "Holy, holy, holy, Lord God Almighty." They never stop, day or night, saying, "Holy, holy, holy, Lord God Almighty..." because in the glory realm, there is the revelation and a knowing of who He is.

> *"For God, who commanded the light to shine out of darkness, hath shined in our hearts, to give the light of the knowledge of the glory of God in the face of Jesus Christ."*
>
> - 2 Corinthians 4:6

The glory releases an anointing to see Him. The glory releases a revelation that comes from the light of the knowledge of the glory of God. It comes from the very face of Jesus Christ. The more we worship Him, the more glory comes, the more we will see.

Scripture says that the knowledge of the glory of God comes from the face of Jesus Christ. Therefore, we must be those who seek His face and see His face. When we see Jesus we are changed. When we stand in His glory we are changed. When we look upon His face we are changed and we have a desire to be like Him. It's in the glory that we see Him and desire to be like Him.

In the glory we can know His compassion. In the glory we can know His love. In the glory we can know His holiness. In the glory we can know His mercy and His grace. In the glory we can know Him. So the Lord wants us to be anointed to see His face.

As we worship, we will learn that the will of God and the purpose of God can be seen in the face of the Lord. When you look at His face, you can know His purpose. You can know His heart. You can know His mind. You can know His desires. If you want to see the heart of God, look into His eyes.

"But as it is written, Eye hath not seen, nor ear heard, neither have entered into the heart of man, the things which God hath prepared for them that love him. But God hath revealed them

unto us by his Spirit: for the Spirit searcheth all things, yea, the deep things of God."
- 1 Corinthians 2:9-10

I believe that God wants us to live in this realm of worship that leads to the revelation of that which eye has not seen nor ear heard and we can only live in that realm as we live in His glory. We don't live in the realm of logic... We live in the realm of glory.

> *"And the glory of the LORD shall be revealed, and all flesh shall see it together: for the mouth of the LORD hath spoken it." - Isaiah 40:5*

The spirit of revelation works in the midst of the revealed glory. The time is coming when all flesh will see the revelation of the glory of God—together!

David wrote this about the King of glory:

> *"Lift up your heads, O ye gates; and be ye lift up, ye everlasting doors; and the King of glory shall come in. Who is this King of glory? The LORD strong and mighty, the LORD mighty in battle. Lift up your heads, O ye gates; even lift them up, ye everlasting doors; and the King of glory shall come in. Who is this King of glory? The LORD of hosts, he is the King of glory. Selah."*
> *- Psalm 24:7-10*

Who is this King of glory? Many of us know Him as Savior, we know Him as Healer, we know Him as Provider. Now we must know Him as the King of glory. Every experience that God allows us to have is for one purpose: To know Him.

One of the meanings for gates in the Old Testament times was a place that controlled access and provided protection. Let's look at it from the aspect of providing access. As we open the gates of our hearts, His glory comes in.

In Psalm 24, the King with his procession is approaching the gate. He asked for entry. The gatekeeper asked, "Who is approaching the gate?" The words are shouted back:

> *"The Lord strong and mighty the Lord mighty in battle."*

This gains Him immediate entry. Who is this King of glory? He is the Lord of hosts. He is the Captain of all the angelic armies, the armies of the nations. The Ruler of everything in heaven and in earth.

When that heavenly portal opens, we allow this King access into our life and into our city through our worship. Open the portals of glory so that He may come in!

There's a portal that opens and releases glory as we worship. In worship, we are changed from glory to glory. We become like Him Who we worship. Therefore

His glory not only indwells us, but is manifested through us.

> *"God hast crowned us with glory."* - Psalm 8:5

> *"A Psalm of David. Give unto the LORD, O ye mighty, give unto the LORD glory and strength. Give unto the LORD the glory due unto his name; worship the LORD in the beauty (GLORY) of holiness (that which is consecrated...set apart) to God."* - Psalm 29:1-2

Glory is directly related to consecrated worship.

In Genesis 28, Jacob dreams a dream:

> *"...and behold a ladder set up on the earth, and the top of it reached to heaven: and behold the angels of God ascending and descending on it. And, behold, the LORD stood above it, and said, I am the LORD God of Abraham thy father, and the God of Isaac: the land whereon thou liest, to thee will I give it, and to thy seed; And thy seed shall be as the dust of the earth, and thou shalt spread abroad to the west, and to the east, and to the north, and to the south: and in thee and in thy seed shall all the families of the earth be blessed. And, behold, I am with thee, and will keep thee in all places whither thou goest, and*

will bring thee again into this land; for I will not leave thee, until I have done that which I have spoken to thee of. And Jacob awaked out of his sleep, and he said, Surely the LORD is in this place; and I knew it not. And he was afraid, and said, How dreadful is this place! this is none other but the house of God, and this is the gate of heaven. And Jacob rose up early in the morning, and took the stone that he had put for his pillows, and set it up for a pillar, and poured oil upon the top of it." - Genesis 28:12-18

In this visitation, God revealed to Jacob that He is the Lord of the past, the present and the future. This brought Jacob up into a new place of relationship with the Lord and Jacob began to worship in a different way.

God Himself was the One that initiated this open portal of glory. The angels ascending and descending is a symbol of what must take place in our lives. First, we have to ascend through our worship. After receiving revelation, experiencing and living in this realm of the glory of God, we descend back into the earth to release God's Kingdom.

We must have the glory to change nations. If His glory is to be revealed in the nations, His glory must first be revealed in each one of us—in our lives. That's why David wrote earlier in Psalm 24:

"Who shall ascend into the hill of the LORD? or who shall stand in his holy place? He that hath clean hands, and a pure heart; who hath not lifted up his soul unto vanity, nor sworn deceitfully. He shall receive the blessing from the LORD, and righteousness from the God of his salvation. This is the generation of them that seek him, that seek thy face, O Jacob. Selah."

- Psalm 24:3-6

As the glory is revealed we will begin to have grace and peace multiplied unto us and the glory of God will work in us to bring forth the excellence of who He is. Worship is the key that will enable us to nurture and release the glory of God.

The Lord wants us to worship in such a way that we embrace His glory. Only then can we move the heart of God. Only then will He release a glory that will bring the manifestation of His glorious presence.

When the glory is manifested, the flesh cannot rule. Daily, God invites us to build an altar of worship that releases the glory of God, gives you His perspective and allows you to see His face.

This is the mandate of our higher call.

Chapter 12

Called for Global Impact: Dancing in the Glory

I was made for glory. You were made for glory. It is a gift from God. Glory is the inheritance of every believer.

The word "glory" is defined as weight, splendor, copiousness, honor or honorable. Only God has true glory. His glory shines brighter than the sun.

Psalm 8 tells us that we are crowned with glory; therefore, we are created to live in the glory of our God—to walk in the glory, talk in the glory, dance in the glory of our God.

> "A Psalm of David. O LORD our Lord, how excellent is thy name in all the earth! who hast set thy glory above the heavens. Out of the mouth of babes and sucklings hast thou ordained strength because of thine enemies, that thou mightest still the enemy and the avenger. When I consider thy heavens, the work of thy fingers, the moon and the stars, which thou hast ordained; What is man, that thou art mindful of him? and the son of man, that thou visitest him? For thou hast made him a little l ower than the angels, and hast crowned him with glory and honour. Thou madest him to have dominion over the works of thy hands; thou hast

put all things under his feet: O LORD our Lord,
how excellent is thy name in all the earth!"
- Psalm 8:1-9

Looking at the story of Psalm 8, David kept his father's sheep. As a young man, he was with the sheep day and night. I believe that as David saw the moon and the stars, he came to know God personally. Therefore, he knew that the strong and powerful God made them all.

David also understood that the enemies of God were against Him and His people. Through his intimate relationship with God and revelation of God's power, he knew that God would fight for His people and make His people strong. God is more powerful than all his enemies. God will always win.

Sometimes the power and grace of God appears wonderfully in those who are most unlikely to rule. The power of God brings to pass great things by very weak and unlikely instruments, that the excellency of the power might more evidently appear to be of God, and not of man. When these unlikely instruments conquer the most powerful and malicious enemies, it confounds adversaries and advances the glory of God

Strength, force, security, majesty, praise, boldness, might and power has been ordained. This He does, because of His enemies, that He may put them to silence.

The majesty and glory of our King makes us want to glorify Him. There are no words that can completely express His excellent greatness. O LORD, our Lord, how excellent is Thy name in all the earth!

His name is powerful, mighty, noble, worthy, great and magnificent! His name is glorious and honorable. Yet, He, the Almighty Sovereign King, sees us, cares for us, and yes, He remembers us and visits us.

God created man for His own glory. Isaiah 43:7 says, *"Even every one that is called by my name: for I have created him for my glory, I have formed him; yea, I have made him."* We were created for His glory. We live, move and have our being in His glory.

God makes the minister and the ministry one. Therefore, every part of our lives is meant to be surrounded, enveloped and crowned with His glory. We are encircled and compassed about, both when we attack the enemies of our soul or when we need protection. This is the revelation we must learn and live to manifest the glory of God that will change hearts and ultimately, change nations.

God has crowned us with glory and honor. The word honor means magnificence, splendor, beauty, comeliness, excellency, majesty and favor. This same God has made us to have dominion over the works of His hands. Dominion means to rule to govern, to reign and to cause to have power. He has caused us to have power.

He has put all things under our feet. Because the Lord is our habitation, He gives His angels charge over us and causes us to tread upon the lion and adder—

upon the young lion and the dragon. Those things that try to oppress us will be overtaken by the glory and our feet then become the oppressor of our enemies.

Through our dance, we trample them under our feet. We dance through troops. Troops are those things that try to press against us or overtake us. But we can leap over walls. He makes our feet like hinds feet, enlarges our steps under us and makes sure that our feet do not slip, shake, or slide so we can be carriers of His glory.

Our enemies fall under our feet. He gives each of us strength for the battle. He subdues under us those that rise up against us. He has also given us the necks of our enemies to dance upon injustice and upon those that desire our destruction.

As we dance in the glory, we take salvation to the nations. This is the higher call. This is our mandate.

> *"For whosoever shall call upon the name of the Lord shall be saved. How then shall they call on him in whom they have not believed? and how shall they believe in him of whom they have not heard? and how shall they hear without a preacher? And how shall they preach, except they be sent? As it is written, How beautiful are the feet of them that preach the gospel of peace, and bring glad tidings of good things!"*
> - Romans 10:13-15

As we dance, our feet preach the gospel of peace. Our feet dance tidings of good things. Wherever our feet go, we carry the presence and the glory of God. This is how the glory of our God will cover the earth as the waters cover the sea. Our dance can create an atmosphere for the glory of His presence to manifest. Through our worship, we build a throne for the King.

The highest form of worship is when we become worship, not just "do" worship. Our lives must reflect the King. As we die to ourselves, we can begin to hear from heaven and dance the dances that He releases from His heart, from His throne. Until then, we have not begun to dance in the glory.

Because we were created to worship, we do not lean to our own understanding. We yield our bodies to God as living sacrifices and allow Him to dance His dances through us. Just as the keys on a keyboard do not move unless someone plays them, so we must yield to Holy Spirit and allow Him to play us like an instrument.

Once we are yielded instruments, God can release His glory. His glory will win every war. In the glory, there is no lack. Healing, deliverance, joy, salvation, and provision will all be released as we dance in the glory. Our regions will be transformed as we dance in the glory.

Glory shifts things. Glory transforms things. Let the glory rule. Think from the glory realm. Live in the glory realm. Dance in the glory realm. To walk, live and dance in the glory means to administrate His government and His Kingdom in the earth realm.

We must remember that the ultimate in worship is the presence of the Lord, not our physical activities. Worship must focus on Him, not on self. Let us cry out for that which is authentic so we do not fill our worship with mere physical activities.

> *"Honour and majesty are before him: strength and beauty are in his sanctuary. Give unto the LORD, O ye kindreds of the people, give unto the LORD glory and strength. Give unto the LORD the glory due unto his name: bring an offering, and come into his courts. O worship the LORD in the beauty of holiness: (fear... twist or whirl in a circular or spiral manner, - dance) before him, all the earth. Say among the heathen that the LORD reigneth: the world also shall be established that it shall not be moved: he shall judge the people righteously." - Psalm 96:6-10*

Rejoice! Jump for joy! God has turned our mourning into dancing! He has put off our sackcloth and girded us with gladness! Our glory will sing praise to Him, and not be silent. We will not hold our peace.

As we surrender to the glory of the King, the impact will be felt globally. I traveled to Korea and 30 days later, I traveled to Haiti. At the time of my visit, two nations could not have been more different, yet both nations were in need of an impact of God's glory.

I found the church in Korea to be alive, filled with joy and expectation, ready to impact their nation with God's glory. In vivid contrast, I experienced many people in Haiti who seemed to be in the throes of a spiritual hurricane, even as they were still recovering from the dramatic trauma of a natural hurricane.

The nations as a whole are in a tumultuous place. Let us dance in Haiti until the stronghold of voodoo is broken and the body of Christ rises up in the splendor of the Lord. Pray for the indigenous people of every nation to rise up in righteousness. Pray for them to go forth and dance in His glory.

Dance in Israel... until the veils are removed from their eyes. Dance before the Lord and give Him no rest, until He establishes and makes Jerusalem a praise in the earth.

Dance in Holland... until righteousness overtakes the land and the ladies of the red light district realize that they were created by a loving God who sees their value and their worth.

Dance in South Africa... until every single remnant of apartheid is completely destroyed.

Dance in Mexico... until every gang member and drug lord is converted and delivered from the kingdom of darkness to the Kingdom of light.

Dance in the glory... until wicked governments are brought down and masses of people rejoice because the righteous have become rulers.

Dance in every nation... until the glory of God fills every kindred, tongue and people.

Dance in the glory... until the kingdoms of this world become the kingdoms of our Lord, and of His Christ. He shall reign forever and ever.

He is the King of glory. Glory in His holy name. Dance in His holy name so the heart of the nations can rejoice as they seek the Lord.

Dance before Him in glory. Be the sight, the sign and the sound. Ascribe to Him, bring to Him the glory that is due His name and dance, all the earth. His Kingdom will be established and His righteousness shall be released.

> *"Glory and honour are in his presence; strength and gladness are in his place. Give unto the LORD, ye kindreds of the people, give unto the LORD glory and strength. Give unto the LORD the glory due unto his name: bring an offering, and come before him: worship the LORD in the*

beauty of holiness. Fear before him, all the earth: the world also shall be stable, that it be not moved. Let the heavens be glad, and let the earth rejoice: and let men say among the nations, The LORD reigneth."

- 1 Chronicles 16:27-31

First, we are told that glory is in His presence. Then, the scripture admonishes us to give, ascribe or bring Him glory. We are to bring an offering as we fall down and worship Him.

The first word in verse 30 is very interesting. The word "fear" is the word chuwl. Strong's Concordance translates it as "to twist or whirl in a circular manner, specifically to dance." Can it be that all the physical earth was created to whirl before the Lord, thereby bringing glory to His name, establishing and stabilizing the inhabitants of the nations?

The same word can also be found in Psalm 90...

"Before the mountains were brought forth, or ever thou hadst formed (chuwl) the earth and the world, even from everlasting to everlasting, thou art God." - Psalm 90:2

Can it be that God Himself whirled in a circular manner (as in dancing) as He created the earth and the inhabitants thereof? You will also find chuwl, in Psalm 29...

"Give unto the LORD the glory due unto his name; worship the LORD in the beauty of holiness. The voice of the LORD is upon the waters: the God of glory thundereth: the LORD is upon many waters. The voice of the LORD is powerful; the voice of the LORD is full of majesty. The voice of the LORD breaketh the cedars; yea, the LORD breaketh the cedars of Lebanon. He maketh them also to skip like a calf; Lebanon and Sirion like a young unicorn. The voice of the LORD divideth the flames of fire. The voice of the LORD shaketh the wilderness; the LORD shaketh the wilderness of Kadesh. The voice of the LORD shaketh (chuwl) the wilderness; the LORD shaketh the wilderness of Kadesh." - Psalm 29:2-8

As we worship Him in the beauty of holiness, this releases the majestic voice of the Lord and brings glory to our dance. Flames of fire attend the voice of God, illuminating our hearts, releasing His glory as a holy flame. His voice is filled with glory and has the ability to dance over our wilderness, breaking down barriers and causing us to jump and leap wildly for joy.

"And the glory which thou gave me I have given them; that they may be one, even as we are one." - John 17:22

He has given us His glory to make us one. We need the glory to be one!

When we worship as one, Psalm 22 tells us that God inhabits the praises of His people. He sets up His throne in the midst of our worship, as Judge. When we worship as one, that's when the worship on earth reflects the worship in heaven. As we worship as one, His judgment is released against our enemies!

"Oh Lord, our Lord, how excellent is Your name in all the earth!" His spiritual weight, His essence, His character, that which makes Him infinite and boundless, with no restrictions, has been given to us to be physical demonstrations of God's glory.

> *"Arise, shine; for thy light is come, and the glory of the LORD is risen upon thee. For, behold, the darkness shall cover the earth, and gross darkness the people: but the LORD shall arise upon thee, and his glory shall be seen upon thee. And the Gentiles shall come to thy light, and kings to the brightness of thy rising. Lift up thine eyes round about, and see: all they gather themselves together, they come to thee: thy sons shall come from far, and thy daughters shall be nursed at thy side. Then thou shalt see, and flow together, and thine heart shall fear, and be enlarged; because the abundance of the sea shall be converted unto thee, the forces of the Gentiles shall come unto thee."* - Isaiah 60:1-5

Arise is a call to stand up! Stir yourself! Shine! Be set on fire! No more movement for the sake of movement.

I call on those who are willing to dance only for one purpose—the purpose of releasing His glory! As you valiantly dance the dances of heaven, may His glory be seen upon you as a visible manifestation. As it is in heaven, let it be in us.

Dance to heal the brokenhearted. Dance deliverance to the captives. Dance the opening of the prison doors. Use the key of God's glory to see nations transformed by the brightness of your rising.

The world will know those who carry His glory. They are waiting for the appearing, the coming, the illumin-ation, the manifestation and revealed revelation of the sons of God. Dancing valiantly in the Sprit, in the glory of God, can have a global impact resulting in revival! Together, we can change the world.

This is the higher call.

CHAPTER 13

Called to Advance the Kingdom of God

Daily, we step into the destiny that God has for us and has planned for us from before the foundations of the earth. God saw you right where you are. Daily, you make a choice to step into purpose.

In every nation, the indigenous people are important. They carry the will of God for that nation. They have a legal position. It is tied to the soil from which they come.

There is a new glory fire on the lampstand of our worship. God is assembling the true worshipers from the nations. Right now, declare an open heaven over your nation. Ask the Lord to send you forth to light the fire. Become a signal fire. A signal fire is a fire on a hill or a tower that can be seen from a distance.

The church must enter into a new season of gathering. We must go from church gatherings to Kingdom gatherings—gatherings that will create a new atmosphere in the earth realm. Our daily prayer must be the prayer "Thy Kingdom come, Thy will be done." The manifestation of God's Kingdom is becoming a reality in the earth. When we see God's will being done, we see His Kingdom being established.

God has been shifting His people out of old structures, including former worship structures. This is the season for a new administration in worship. This is the season of the watchman and this is the season when the eyes of the Lord are upon His house. God is looking to see how His people are watching and worshiping in His house in this season.

We are in a season where new doors are opening for God's people. It is time for the prosperity that was lost in the last season to be restored. It's time for the promises to manifest to a people who are prepared and positioned.

We are in a time when we will see the reigning church arise. The worship of the reigning church has to do with who will win the war for the atmosphere and territory. We must go higher in worship. We must go to the mountain of God to advance His Kingdom.

> "And it shall come to pass in the last days, that the mountain of the LORD'S house shall be established in the top of the mountains, and shall be exalted above the hills; and all nations shall flow unto it." - Isaiah 2:2

We are His dwelling place on earth. Our prayer must be as in heaven, so in earth. We are already seated in heavenly places so let's see from the throne; from a position of rulership.

His dwelling place is the highest place—Zion. As His people, we come up to the mountain of the Lord. When we do this, every other mountain will look small. If we ascend to the mountain of the Lord, He will restore perspective, vision and truth. For too long we have looked at other mountains—mountains of depression, disease, problems, weaknesses, disappointments, lone-liness and fear.

The time is now for us to come up to the highest mountain, Zion, God's dwelling place. We will see, we will hear and we will know. From this place He will establish our heart.

> *"Blessed are they that dwell in thy house: they will be still praising thee. Selah. Blessed is the man whose strength is in thee; in whose heart are the ways of them."* - Psalm 84:4-5

Your heart shall be a highway to Zion. You will be His dwelling place. The nations will be connected from this place. The hour is here now. He has handpicked us for this time. Come up, meet Him face to face. Our answer must be, "Lord, we are coming. We are ready." From the place of readiness, we advance His Kingdom.

> *"And from the days of John the Baptist until now the Kingdom of Heaven suffers violence, and the violent take it by force."* - Matthew 11:12

The key to advancing the Kingdom is to pray as Jesus told us to pray: "Thy Kingdom come, Thy will be done in earth, as it is in heaven." When we read the words, "forcefully advancing," "forceful men lay hold," "suffers violence" and "the violent take it by force," it might sound like violent men using force to advance the Kingdom of God. That's what the disciples wanted Jesus to do. They wanted to kill all the Romans.

These images of forceful men are not what many of us were raised with in regards to Christianity. As a matter of fact, many of us were never taught anything at all regarding the advancing of the Kingdom of God. What we were taught is that this Kingdom is one of love, peace, care, compassion, and mercy. And it is. Just be nice to everyone all the time. So how can we reconcile taking it by force with love? Are they both correct? Yes.

It is not just about being violent or forceful. It is about being passionate and desperate for God in our desire to advance the Kingdom of God so that others may experience the same relationship with Jesus Christ that we experience. It's about being a passionate worshiper, willing to lay your life down, taking God at His Word, walking in His authority, not leaning to your own understanding and not compromising in any area. The truth is that if you compromise in one area of your life, you are likely to compromise in other areas.

That word "violence" denotes "a strength, vigor, earnestness of desire and endeavor." It also shows us what fervency and zeal are required of all those who purpose to seize and advance the Kingdom. The Kingdom of heaven was never intended to indulge the easy life. God is not interested in your comfort. He is interested in seeing you conform to Kingdom culture.

The Kingdom is not for the faint of heart or for those looking for an easy road. It is for those who are willing to do whatever is necessary, press past the norm and be whatever is necessary in order to advance and grow God's Kingdom here on earth.

We must choose to be a violent, Kingdom enforcer. There is a shaking and a shifting taking place in the body of Christ. There is a stirring in His people, a discontent with church as usual. His call is for us to step out of mediocrity and into the fullness of His call. In these last days, the resurrection, life-giving power that was in the second Adam, Jesus Christ, will be seen in His sons.

God has called you by name at a strategic time in history. He has put you in a strategic place for His purposes. It does not matter what has happened to you in the past. You are here right now!

Each one of you is needed. Each person is important for the plan of God for this region. Do not buy the lie that you are not needed. The Bible says that every joint supplies. The thigh bone cannot say to the knee, "I don't need you."

We each have a prophetic destiny to fulfill and we need each person do the part God has called them to do. Advancing the Kingdom will require us to become a more disciplined people under His dominion. No more living day to day, not knowing the destiny and progressive purpose of God in our lives.

We must shift. The shift will take us from what we have known to what God knows. We must expect higher, surrender higher, believe higher. This is the season of exponential growth. We must connect with people of like belief, like surrender, and like faith. Connect with those who are willing to go to the same level of sacrifice. Disconnect from those who refuse to shift.

Looking again at this scripture, Satan is willing and has no reservations concerning the use of violence and force in war against the Kingdom of Heaven and its citizens. We are to meet Satan's violence and forceful attempts to destroy God's Kingdom with even greater violence and force in thanksgiving, prayer, worship, faith and love.

The words of Jesus from Luke 10:

> *"And he said unto them, I beheld Satan as lightning fall from heaven. Behold, I give unto you power to tread on serpents and scorpions, and over all the power of the enemy: and nothing shall by any means hurt you."*
>
> - Luke 10:18-19

When we read such things as, "tread on snakes and scorpions," "overcome all the power of the enemy," "wage war," "demolish strongholds, arguments and every pretension," "put on the full armor of God," "take your stand," and "stand your ground," we should understand that to go to war against Satan and his kingdom will demand the meeting of violence with violence and force with force. It's time to take the Kingdom by force.

> *"When Jesus came into the region of Caesarea Philippi, He asked His disciples, saying, 'Who do men say that I, the Son of Man, am?'"*
>
> *- Matthew 16:13*

> *"So they said, 'Some say John the Baptist, some Elijah, and others Jeremiah or one of the prophets.' He said to them, 'But who do you say that I am?' Simon Peter answered and said, 'You are the Christ, the Son of the living God.' Jesus answered and said to him, 'Blessed are you, Simon Bar-Jonah, for flesh and blood has not revealed this to you, but My Father who is in heaven. And I also say to you that you are Peter, and on this rock I will build My church, and the gates of Hades shall not prevail against it. And I will give you the keys of the kingdom of heaven, and whatever you bind on earth will be bound in heaven, and whatever you loose on earth will be loosed[d] in heaven.'"* - Matthew 16:14-18

That's where we come in. In verse 18, the word "church" is not a religious term. The word is more accurately translated as ekklesia. It is a governmental term meaning called out ones. It's used to refer to a senate—those chosen by the government (cabinet members) in Bible days. Their job was to know the mind of the king, (Caesar)—receive his thoughts, his desires, his passion and his intent, then turn it into legislation that can be implemented for the kingdom. That's the master key! Stay in close contact with the King. Listen to His instructions, then obey.

This ekklesia has been trusted with information critical to the operation of the Kingdom. Even hell itself cannot prevail against it.

> *"And God said, Let us make man in our image, after our likeness: and let them have dominion over the fish of the sea, and over the fowl of the air, and over the cattle, and over all the earth, and over every creeping thing that creepeth upon the earth."* - Genesis 1:26

Dominion means to rule and reign. So as His ekklesia, we are called to operate on another level, unlike the world. We have access to power of the throne. It is a throne of grace. We have been invited and instructed to come boldly. We have already passed from death to life! The same spirit that raised Christ from the dead dwells in us!

CALLED TO ADVANCE THE KINGDOM OF GOD

Let us live in the reality that the One with all power and authority in heaven gave us dominion, access to the throne and keys to His Kingdom! He has given us keys to unlock the Kingdom, take authority, exercise dominion and access all of heaven's resources.

All authority is given to us! Let's raise our level of expectation and stop looking for earthly solutions. Our mandate is to know the times and the seasons of God in these last days. According to Matthew 28, God has given this ekklesia power:

> "And Jesus came and spake unto them, saying, All power is given unto me in heaven and in earth. Go ye therefore, and teach all nations, baptizing them in the name of the Father, and of the Son, and of the Holy Ghost: Teaching them to observe all things whatsoever I have commanded you: and, lo, I am with you alway, even unto the end of the world. Amen."
>
> - Matthew 28:18-20

The word "power" means ability, privilege, force, capacity, competency, freedom, superhuman, potentate, token of control or delegated influence. It also means authority, jurisdiction, liberty, power, right and strength. With this superhuman power and authority, our mandate is to be a wise company of legislators whose only agenda is to advance the Kingdom of God.

Obedience to our King is no longer an option. Obedience must become a mandatory lifestyle.

We do not apologize for who we are, nor do we hide or shrink back in fear. The world will hear His voice through us. We must shift from doing church to being the church with authority and dominion. This is our mandate. It is no longer about us, it is always and only about Him.

God is saying, "I need someone to be my voice. I need someone who is bold as a lion for my Kingdom. I need somebody to cry out for the harvest of lost souls. I need someone who will say here am I, send me."

Dr. Myles Munroe says it this way. "We are in the Kingdom, representing the King of heaven, and we have the keys, yet we are in a war. We are in a culture war. Culture is what defines people. It is the entire way of life of a people group—their beliefs, attitudes, food, clothing, language, government and education."

Every people group has a culture that defines it. There are cultures within cultures. Even so, there is a culture that defines Kingdom advancers. What defines Kingdom culture?

> *"But the fruit of the Spirit is love, joy, peace, longsuffering, gentleness, goodness, faith, Meekness, temperance: against such there is no law."* - Galatians 5:22-23

"For the fruit of the Spirit is in all goodness and righteousness and truth; Proving what is acceptable unto the Lord. And have no fellowship with the unfruitful works of darkness, but rather reprove them." - Ephesians 5:9-11

Our culture is faithfulness, humility and righteousness. The righteous are as bold as a lion (Proverbs 28:1). We do not live or operate in a Kingdom of lies, hatred, sadness, fear, guilt, shame, timidity. Our culture is one of signs, wonders and miracles.

Some of our culture is learned behavior. The culture of the Kingdom must always supersede our learned culture if it is opposite to the Kingdom of God. The culture war is won by those who, with transformed minds, are led by the Spirit of God.

"And be not conformed to this world: but be ye transformed (changed) by the renewing of your mind." - Romans 12:2

Why must we be transformed into Kingdom advancers? Because the world is waiting for us!

"For the earnest expectation of the creation waiteth (expecting, looking) for the manifestation (revelation) of the sons of God."
- Romans 8:19

The world is waiting for the body of Christ to figure out who we are. They are waiting for you.

There is a shaking and a shifting taking place in the body of Christ. There is a stirring in His people, a discontent with church as usual. His call is for us to step out of mediocrity and into the fullness of His call. In these last days, the power that was in the second Adam, Jesus Christ, will be seen in His sons.

The world is waiting for the sons. We are in all areas of society with His keys to reflect His image. The world needs us. God wants the church to understand that we are the ekklesia, the governing voice of God in the earth.

We must arise. We must think governmentally. We do not shift to the ways of the world, they must shift to the ways of our God.

This is the season, the hour, the day, the time of the restored ekklesia. We must arise to advance the Kingdom.

This is our mandate.

Chapter 14

Rule in the Midst of Your Enemies

"A Psalm of David. The LORD said unto my Lord, Sit thou at my right hand, until I make thine enemies thy footstool." - Psalm 110:1

Footstool means to stamp upon.

"The LORD shall send the rod of thy strength out of Zion: rule thou in the midst of thine enemies."
- Psalm 110:2

The word "rod" is the word mattah, meaning a branch (as extending); a tribe; also a rod, whether for chastising correction), ruling (a sceptre), throwing (a lance), or walking (a staff), a support of life,--rod, staff, tribe.

The word "strength" means force, security, majesty, praise. It also means boldness, loud, might, power, strength, strong.

"Rule" means to tread down. It means to have dominion, to prevail against, to reign, to rule or to take over. Where are we called to rule? In the midst of our enemies. We do not wrestle with flesh and blood, but with principalities and powers.

"Thy people shall be willing in the day of thy power, in the beauties of holiness from the womb of the morning: thou hast the dew of thy youth." - Psalm 110:3

God's people are to be a congregated unit. Specifically, a tribe, hence troops or attendants. It also means a flock or a nation of people.

"Power" is the word CHAYIL. It means from a force, an army, wealth, virtue, valor, strength:--able, activity, army, band of men (soldiers), company, (great) forces, goods, host, might, power, riches, strength, strong, substance, train, valiant, valor, virtuous, war, worthy.

Here is what we are seeing. After Jesus conquered sin and death, and rose from the dead, He returned to the Father. And the Father said, "Sit at My right hand, till I make Your enemies Your footstool." So the throne attitude of Jesus is to sit and expect His Father to bring all His defeated enemies under His feet. We need a throne attitude.

Let's look at these scriptures again..

"A Psalm of David. The LORD (Jehovah, the self existent One) ...said unto my Lord, (Adonai, ruler, sovereign, controller and master) Sit (as JUDGE, in ambush) thou at my right hand..."
                                                    - Psalm 110:1

Sit as JUDGE...

> *"The Lord inhabits the praises of His people.*
> *- Psalm 22:3*

"Inhabits" is the word Yashah, meaning He comes to dwell in and to sit as Judge.

God enthrones Himself in our praises and when He comes, the manifested power of His throne of judgment and righteousness also comes. It is a throne of grace to us, but a throne of judgment against our enemies. Therefore, when we praise and when we worship the King, this brings the government of heaven into the earth realm.

> *...until I make thine enemies thy footstool.*
> *- Psalm 110:1*

In biblical times, defeated enemies were brought back in chains and the victorious king would sit on his throne and put his feet upon the backs of his defeated enemies as a sign of victory. Likewise, Jesus' conquered enemies are being dragged to Him one by one, and put under His feet.

> *"And having spoiled principalities and powers, he made a shew of them openly, triumphing over them in it."* - Colossians 2:15

"He raised Him from the dead and seated Him at His right hand... God placed all things under His feet and appointed Him to be head over everything for the church, which is His body..."

- Ephesians 1:20, 22-23

We, the church, are the body of Christ. Who is the one who makes the enemies our footstool? God Himself! He is telling us to have the same throne attitude as Jesus—sit, while He makes our enemies our footstool. All things, including the defeated enemies of disease, poverty, depression and all kinds of curses, are under our feet.

Sitting implies resting. God wants us to rest from striving, rest from trying to figure it out on your own. Rest from our labors. Enter into a place of rejoicing and praise, rest in His finished work. Our mandate is to have a throne attitude! Rule!

Sit at my right hand...

To sit at the right hand of an earthly king was a place of honor, a place of special trust and authority because of the relationship with the king. It was something that was understood without needing explanation at the time.

If you were seated at the right hand of the king, it meant that you could act with his authority. Those who came to you would treat you with respect and obedience, as if you were the king himself.

> *"The LORD shall send the rod of thy strength out of Zion: rule thou in the midst of thine enemies. Thy people shall be willing in the beauties of holiness from the womb of the morning: thou hast the dew of thy youth."* - Psalm 110:2-3

God's people went to Him as a nation, collectively, not as individuals. They said, "WE will do. WE will be willing."

Let commitment shape your understanding. Don't let your understanding shape your commitment. You might not always understand everything. If you try to understand it all, you will never commit to be willing.

God's people shall be willing. Willing to do what? They shall be willing while others are unwilling. They shall be willing to voluntarily consecrate themselves for the service of the King. The simple term "willing" is very expressive. God's people must be willing to die unto all sin and willing to crucify the old man in order that the new man may be formed in them.

They must be willing to be weaned from their own thoughts and purposes, that the thoughts and purposes of God may be fulfilled in them. And when they are willing, God will beautify them with salvation, because there is nothing in them to hinder His working.

They will be a wise, strong, powerful people, led by the Spirit of God who works in us to will and to do of His good pleasure... making us like Himself, to rule in the midst of our enemies. Throne attitude!

I am one of the "willing people." Are you? This "willingness" is the essence of holiness; it constitutes "the beauty of holiness" because the beauty of Christ is released through His willing ones. This is the higher call.

When we surrender to the higher call, we are adorned with the beautiful and glorious robes of right-eousness and true holiness. The dew—that is, thy offspring (the members of the body of Christ) shall be more numerous than the drops of the morning dew.

This is the day of His power! This is the day of His Chayil, powerful, forceful worshiping warriors to arise to their rest, knowing we are already seated in heavenly places. It means learning to rule from heavenly places.

> *"To the intent that now unto the principalities and powers in heavenly places might be known by the church the manifold wisdom of God."*
> - Ephesians 3:10

In order to rule in the midst of our enemies, we must come up higher... NOW!

I was traveling by air. The pilot said, "please fasten your seat belts. We are about to descend." God spoke to my heart that as we stay up higher, seated with Him, resting and ruling, we will not be entangled with the affairs of this life.

We must come to a higher place in our thinking. This will allow us to come to a higher place in our freedom—a higher place in our joy! We are seated there, now! It's only when we "descend" that we are caught by the snare of the enemy and distracted by the cares of this world. No more low-level thinking, no more low-level warfare.

> *"No man that warreth entangleth himself with the affairs of this life; that he may please him who hath chosen him to be a soldier."*
>
> - 2 Timothy 2:4

We must understand this. God says, "My army is filled with wounded soldiers. I send you out to heal them, to lift them up, to empower them, to give them life and set them free. Remind them who they are. Remind them who I created them to be. You were once wounded but I have healed your wounds. Now go heal others. Set them free." This is the higher call.

We are sent to bring permanent change. We will rule in the midst of our enemies. Allow the full power of God to sit as Judge as we praise Him and allow Him to be enthroned upon our praises.

> *"In that day will I raise up the tabernacle of David that is fallen, and close up the breaches*

thereof; and I will raise up his ruins, and I will build it as in the days of old: That they may possess the remnant of Edom, and of all the heathen, which are called by my name, saith the LORD that doeth this." - Amos 9:11-12

The tabernacle of David was the place where worship was first set in order. The word "possess" means to occupy by driving out the previous tenant. It means to cast out, to consume, to destroy, to disinherit.

Our praise and worship is a weapon against the enemy. An ambush is a surprise attack by people lying in wait in a concealed position. Praise and worship is the surprise ambush!

The enemy wants you to sit around and cry when you face difficult situations. But God says, "Come up higher. I have already seated you in heavenly places with Me. I have raised you up to possess. Now praise because it causes you to rule in the midst of your enemies. Praise allows Me to fight on your behalf."

We see this pattern throughout the Word of God. The root of the word Chayil is the word Chuwl, meaning to dance—to whirl in a circular manner. The first mention of dance is in Exodus 15:20. God delivered the children of Israel from many years in bondage to Pharaoh and delivered them through the Red Sea. This represents the fact that we have been brought through the blood of Jesus and delivered from death, hell, sin, sickness and the grave itself.

Miriam, the prophetess, led the women in the dance, (chuwl, company of dancers) with singing and with a tambourine. She was the one who led the dance because of her relationship to the deliverer. The custom was for the closest female relative to meet or greet the returning victor after they had won a battle. That's us! We are the closest female relative to our returning victor, Jesus Christ! Their dance was a surprise ambush dance of deliverance. Our dance is a surprise ambush dance of deliverance!

This could not have been the first time Miriam and the children of Israel danced. Dance had been handed from one generation to another. At this point in history, the dance of deliverance was done in the midst of their enemies. You say, but I thought they were all dead! They were! Exodus 14:30 says:

> *"Thus the LORD saved Israel that day out of the hand of the Egyptians; and Israel saw the Egyptians dead upon the sea shore."*

The horse and its rider had been thrown into the sea. The enemies they had seen would not be seen again!

David danced and even though he was the king, he was criticized! Sometimes the enemy is in your own family, and in your own house.

> *"And it came to pass, as the ark of the covenant of the LORD came to the city of David, that*

Michal the daughter of Saul looking out at a window saw king David dancing and playing: and she despised him in her heart."

- 1 Chronicles 15:29

In the end, David ruled over all of Israel and in the midst of his enemies.

It is reported that Jesus danced with His disciples at the last supper. He was then betrayed and ultimately crucified. The devil thought he had won.

"Which none of the princes of this world knew: for had they known it, they would not have crucified the Lord of glory." - 1 Corinthians 2:8

But He rose on the third day and now He sits at the right hand of the Father. He forever rules in the midst of His enemies!

God wants us to live lives of surrender to the Father so we can also live resurrected lives, revealing and reflecting the Father, showing forth the praises of Him who has called us out of darkness into His marvelous light!

This is our mandate. This is the higher call!

Conclusion

Called to Be a New Wineskin

"And no man putteth new wine into old bottles; else the new wine will burst the bottles, and be spilled, and the bottles shall perish. But new wine must be put into new bottles; and both are preserved. No man also having drunk old wine straightway desireth new: for he saith, The old is better." - Luke 5:37-39

If you keep drinking the old wine you won't desire the new. You will keep thinking that the old is ok. If you keep living the same way, thinking the same way, acting the same way, dancing the same way, you cannot answer the higher call.

Evaluate your life. When confronted with a situation, if you address it the same way you always have, ask yourself if you are ready to receive the new wine, to become a new wineskin. Don't resort to your old ways. With the new wineskin mentality comes authority, revelation and direction.

Answer the call. Let go of the old. Release old attitudes. Let go of old ways. Let the old mentality go! Fear must go! Lack of confidence must go! Selfishness must go! You can't do the old and expect the new. Choose to embrace the new. He will pour in new wine.

John the Baptist preached a necessary and relevant message as a forerunner of Jesus. When the time came for Jesus to begin His ministry, John had to decrease so the ministry of Jesus could increase. It was time for a new wineskin. The followers of John had to shift. They had no choice. We have no choice but to shift. We must decrease so the ministry of Jesus Christ can increase and have its full power. This is our higher call.

The higher call of the new wineskin will change your life and the lives of those you touch. As you receive the new wine, you can pour out new wine.

> *"And as they departed, Jesus began to say unto the multitudes concerning John, What went ye out into the wilderness to see? A reed shaken with the wind? But what went ye out for to see? A man clothed in soft raiment? behold, they that wear soft clothing are in kings' houses. But what went ye out for to see? A prophet? yea, I say unto you, and more than a prophet. For this is he, of whom it is written, Behold, I send my messenger before thy face, which shall prepare thy way before thee."* - Matthew 11:7-10

Jesus asked the people what they went to see. Did they go to see "a reed shaken with the wind?" He may have been referring to John's gestures and actions in preaching. Perhaps John might have waved to and fro as a reed does, when shaken by the wind. Did the people go to see him move his body to and fro? Was it not to hear his message and receive from God?

When people see you minister God's messages in movement, do they only see your actions and gestures or do they receive from the heart of God? Jesus let them know that if actions and gestures was what they were looking for, they were mistaken.

John was firm and stable in his message and ministry. He did not have one message while preaching and live another message in his daily life. The testimony he lived was always consistent with himself. He was always the same.

Did the people understand what they went to see? Were they looking for the softness of a reed, the luxury of a man in fine clothes or the power of a prophet? Did they go to be entertained or to hear the Word of the Lord? We are not called to entertain. We are called to reveal Christ.

"What did you come to see? A reed shaking in the wind?" This was spoken of John the Baptist and now God is speaking it to you. "You have been shaken like a reed blowing in the wind. You have not been broken except in your brokenness before Me. Though you will experience shaking, you are strong and you will not break. You will minister and serve people whose lives are shaking. Offer your life to Me in brokenness. And when people see you they will look past you and see Me."

We must be the sights... revealing Him and Him alone.

We must be the signs... Our gestures and actions must convey divine information and instructions.

We must be the sounds... making sure we are conveying only the specific impressions we have heard while in His presence.

This is our higher call.

DR. PAMELA HARDY

Dr. Pamela Hardy is an ordained minister, a preacher and teacher of the Word of God. She received a Master of Fine Arts degree and a Doctor of Ministry degree from FICU in Merced, California.

Pamela has danced on Broadway in New York City and performed in national and regional touring productions.

Dr. Hardy travels throughout the United States and abroad. God has sent her as an Ambassador to over 20 countries, including Scotland, Germany, Nicaragua, Panama, Ecuador, South Africa, Israel, Malaysia, England, Canada, Costa Rica, Mexico, Suriname, Fiji, Holland, Korea and throughout the Caribbean.

She serves as Vice President of Chayil Women International, a global network focused on empowering women and changing lives. She is also co-owner of Basar Publishing Company. BPC is devoted to publishing the good news of Jesus Christ through advancing the ministry of the arts. She is the author of "Let the Nations Rejoice, An Invitation to Dance," "Act NOW!" and is a contributing author for "Every Knee Shall Bow," a literary compilation of international voices speaking on the importance of the movement arts, as well as an inspirational book for women entitled, "Dream Again: Awakening The Dreamer Inside Of You."

Dr. Hardy is the host of Global Horizons, an Internet Program focused on worship in the nations, and founder of Eagles International Training Institute, a mentoring program for those in dance ministry. EITI has a presence in over 20 countries. She also gives apostolic oversight to the EITI International Business Institute, Prophetic School, Flag Institute, Prayer Institute, Mime, Leadership Institute, Company of Prophets, School of Worship, Mime Institute, Authors Institute, Pageantry Institute, EITI Torah School, Drama School, Technique Center, TEN (The Eagles Network – Worldwide) and EITI Children.

She serves in leadership with her husband Christopher at Kingdom Ambassadors Global Impact Center and is also a member at Glory of Zion International under Apostle Chuck Pierce.

The prophetic anointing that is on her life will bring an increase in vision and will challenge and motivate others to be released into destiny and purpose. She is the Founder and Director of **Set Free Evangelistic Ministries.**

Contact Information:
Phone: **214-402-9647**   Email: **drpamelahardy@aol.com**
Websites: **www.drpamelahardy.org** / **www.eaglesiti.org**

OTHER BOOKS BY DR. PAMELA HARDY

ACT NOW! 31 Nuggets to ACTIVATE, CULTIVATE and TRANSFORM Your World! A Devotional Journal

and

Let the Nations Rejoice!

Purchase books, DVDs, and training materials:

www.drpamelahardy.org